Redemption

Redemption

Faith, Justice, and Sisterhood on Death Row

Lawrence Wright

ALFRED A. KNOPF New York
2026

A BORZOI BOOK
FIRST HARDCOVER EDITION
PUBLISHED BY ALFRED A. KNOPF 2026

Published by Alfred A. Knopf, a division of Penguin Random House LLC, 1745 Broadway, New York, NY 10019.

Knopf, Borzoi Books, and the colophon are registered trademarks of Penguin Random House LLC.

Library of Congress Cataloging-in-Publication Data
Names: Wright, Lawrence, 1947– author
Title: Redemption : faith, justice, and sisterhood on death row / Lawrence Wright.
Description: First hardcover edition. | New York, NY : Alfred A. Knopf, 2026.
Identifiers: LCCN 2025054402 | ISBN 9780593805084 hardcover | ISBN 9780593805091 ebook
Subjects: LCSH: Women death row inmates—Texas | Women death row inmates—Religious life—Texas | Church work with prisoners—Catholic Church | Capital punishment—Texas | Criminal justice, Administration of—Texas | LCGFT: Case studies
Classification: LCC HV8699.U6 T498 2026
LC record available at https://lccn.loc.gov/2025054402

penguinrandomhouse.com | aaknopf.com

Printed in the United States of America
1st Printing

The authorized representative in the EU for product safety and compliance is Penguin Random House Ireland, Morrison Chambers, 32 Nassau Street, Dublin D02 YH68, Ireland, https://eu-contact.penguin.ie.

To Justice

Foreword

Reporters are skeptics by nature, and religious belief falls into a category we rarely explore, except when scandal leaps onto the stage. I rarely use theological language, and I skirt religious explanations for human events. Even the idea of "redemption" is charged for me, a cousin of the term "salvation," from which I keep my distance. So this book posed a challenge.

As an adult I've made episodic forays into various expressions of faith, although I've never returned to the fervent beliefs I held as a teenager. My main interest has been as a journalist. I started with the *Race Relations Reporter,* in Nashville, covering the civil rights movement, where I witnessed the transformative power of faith in the lives of people who made America a fairer and more just society. I've written about the Amish, Mormons, Scientologists, Satanists, Baptists, Catholics, Pentecostals, atheists, and my own Methodist upbringing. After 9/11, I spent five years wandering through the Arab world and South Asia, talking to deeply religious Muslims who longed to be martyred in their quest to destroy America. What I've learned from this journalistic odyssey is that strong political views may scarcely affect behavior, but powerful religious beliefs can rule a person's life. Religion is a transformative force, for good or ill, and almost impossible to tame when it reaches deep.

The question that arises from death row is whether a condemned person who has been transformed by religion should have to die for the crime he or she committed in another incarnation. I've been in many prisons in my career, and I've observed the power of faith in remodeling the character of people thought to be unredeemable. The sincerity of their reformation is hard to measure, especially within prison walls, but fundamental change is rarely achieved by any other means. It's almost always the case that by the time the executioner puts an end to the discussion years or even decades have passed, the families of the victims have grown old or passed away, and the crimes themselves have been forgotten. Typically, the prisoner who is being led to the gurney has already served most of what would have been a life sentence.

In 1972 the Supreme Court overturned the use of the death penalty, in a case styled *Furman v. Georgia,* because it violated constitutional protections against cruel and unusual punishment. At the time, there were nearly 700 inmates on death rows across the country who suddenly had their sentences commuted to life in prison. The decision was controversial even on the court: Five of the nine justices concurred in the majority opinion, but none of them agreed with the reasoning of the others; and among the four dissenters, two who personally opposed the death penalty thought it was constitutional. In his dissent, Justice William Brennan argued that "the calculated killing of a human being by the State involves, by its very nature, a denial of the executed person's humanity." Such an individual has "lost the right to have rights."

It was the capriciousness of the death penalty that most offended the court. "These death sentences are cruel and unusual in the same way that being struck by lightning is cruel and unusual," Justice Potter Stewart wrote. Justice Thurgood Marshall pointed out that innocent people were always at risk: "No matter how careful courts are, the possibility of perjured testimony, mistaken honest testimony and human error remain too real." Discrimination was certainly at play, as evidenced by the indefensible racial imbalance in sentencing; the ultimate penalty wasn't imposed frequently enough to have any plausible deterrent effect; and the punishment was so far detached from the offense that it lost the sense of righteous retribution at the core of popular support for execution. The final act was the consequence of some slow-moving morbid bureaucracy set in motion decades before. The Supreme Court did not, however, hold that capital punishment was unconstitutional by its very nature, only that its application was haphazard and irrational.

Opponents of the penalty hoped that the court would finally put the issue to rest in its 1976 decision in *Gregg v. Georgia,* which addressed revised laws contrived by thirty-five states and the federal government to comply with *Furman*. Those revised guidelines required juries to consider mitigating circumstances in a separate punishment phase, and death sentences to be automatically reviewed by a higher court. The justices were awed by the massive and immediate revision of state laws to bring the penalty back from the legal grave many Americans thought it had been buried in. "The most marked indication of society's endorsement of the death penalty for murder is the legislative response to *Furman,*" the court noted. Americans had made up their minds that they wanted the option of capital punishment, and the court was not going to stand against popular opinion.

The following year the moratorium on executions was broken by a firing squad in Utah, which put to death Gary Gilmore, who had murdered two men only seventeen days after the court restored capital punishment. Gilmore's last words, as a hood was placed over his head, were "*Dominus vobiscum*" (The Lord be with you), and a Catholic priest responded, "*Et cum spiritu tuo*" (And with your spirit) as he administered last rites.

A few months after the *Gregg* decision, I wrote an article about three men awaiting execution in Georgia. They were Wayne Coleman; his younger half-brother, Carl Isaacs; and George Dungee. They had escaped together from a prison in Maryland and went on a crime spree as they headed to Florida in a stolen car. The object was to see the ocean. Along the way, they picked up Carl and Wayne's fifteen-year-old brother, William "Billy" Isaacs, who would later testify against them. As they passed through Seminole County, in southern Georgia, hoping to steal some gas, they stopped at a farmstead because they thought they saw a pump. It turned out to be an irrigation pump.

The men decided they would rob the mobile home on the property, which was empty when they arrived, but during the burglary the farmers who lived there, all members of the locally prominent Alday clan, began returning from the fields. One by one, five men all together, were shot dead as they entered the trailer. George Dungee, the getaway man who couldn't drive, sat in the car while the killings were underway. Mary Alday, twenty-six, the wife of one of the Alday sons, was raped on the kitchen floor by Carl Isaacs; then the men drove her to a wooded area, where George Dungee raped her, tortured her, and shot her twice in the back.

America has always been a venue for aimless killers, roaming the countryside or the city streets, governed by impulses rather than reason, warring against order, civility, and society itself. When they are finally brought to justice they pose a puzzle for the citizens who are asked to decide their fate. It is one thing to see villains on television, another to encounter them in a courtroom, where they are no longer menacing but exotic, enigmatic creatures, yanked out of our nightmares and made pathetically real. The three men were tried one after the other. As the story of the murders unfolded what would impress each of the juries was the killers' lack of remorse. During his trial, Wayne sat at the defense table reading about himself in a true-crime magazine. The article was titled "Too Evil to Be Called Animals."

Back then, in Georgia, prison visits were rather casual. I sat in a small, windowless room in the Reidsville prison, and the three convicted murderers were brought to me separately: no handcuffs, no chains, no guard, not even a desk between us. They seemed interested but untroubled by their crimes, and happy to tell their stories. George was a diminutive, intellectually handicapped, bisexual Black man. He was extremely nearsighted; in court, he squinted to see the jury because he was not allowed his glasses. He was thirty-five when he decided to escape from the Maryland prison with Carl and Wayne. He had one month remaining on his eighteen-month sentence for failure to pay child support.

Wayne and Carl came from a large, violent, dysfunctional family, and each began committing petty crimes almost as soon as they could walk. Wayne, the oldest—twenty-six when the murders occurred—was redheaded, slight, extremely pale, with tattoos running up his arms that I compared to painted ivory candlesticks. He had nine teeth in his mouth, and stooping shoulders. He could have been a model for Havelock Ellis, the British psychologist, who in 1899 catalogued the features of a born criminal: wizened before his time, scanty beard, voluminous projecting ears, and a cadaverous pallor from "habitual cerebral congestion." His brother, Carl, on the other hand, was darkly handsome, with long black eyelashes, a pretty boy who had been raped in the prison he escaped from.

Wayne was impatient with Carl, who was seven years younger and blamed their mother for their problems. Wayne said that she was in fact "happy-go-lucky." He showed me his "Mom" tattoo. "There are many people in this world," Wayne philosophized, in regards to Carl, "who tend to blame their parents when met with misfortunes, and lands behind prison walls . . . But this particular individual's actions and hardships he brings on himself."

All three men were sentenced to death, but in 1985 the U.S. Court of Appeals overturned their convictions because of the prejudicial atmosphere of the community where they were tried. Each was tried again. Carl Isaacs was convicted and received another death sentence. Wayne Coleman was convicted of all six murders but the jury was unable to reach a decision on execution, so he was sentenced to six consecutive life sentences. George Dungee, who I suspected was in love with Carl, pled guilty to all charges after prosecutors said they were prevented from seeking a death sentence because of his intellectual disabilities. He would die of congestive heart failure in prison. Wayne remains incarcerated as of this writing. Carl was finally executed, by lethal injection, in 2003, twenty-seven years after the murders.

I mention this now-ancient crime because my opinion of the death penalty was affected by that experience. I could see that George Dungee was a hapless follower with diminished intellectual capacity; it would have been barbarous to execute him. I didn't feel that way about Carl and Wayne. I felt justice would be served by their execution.

As I write, the yearslong decline of executions has abruptly reversed course, with forty-seven in 2024, nearly double that of the year before, and the upward trend continues. This book doesn't solve the moral dilemmas posed by capital punishment, although through my reporting on the seven women on Texas death row I have lost faith in the presumption that Texas, or any state, has a system of justice that is sufficiently reliable, fair, or just to assume the power to take a life. Yes, there are an ample number of cases, like the one I just related, where there is no doubt of guilt, but that same system can be subverted by crooked prosecutors, incompetent attorneys, or racial prejudice—as will be shown in the narrative that follows.

And who are these women that we, the state, intend to kill? Most of the women portrayed here are grandmothers who committed their crimes when they were in their late teens or early twenties. I'm not arguing that they are harmless or that they should be paroled into society, although I question the guilt of some of them. Nor am I suggesting that legal safeguards be short-circuited to speed the journey to the death chamber; too many wrongful convictions have been overturned in the painstaking appeals process. What troubles me is that the person on the gurney with the IV in her vein is in profound ways not the same as the young woman with blood on her hands decades ago.

The reader may consider this the final appeal of seven women on Texas death row. It is not a legal appeal; in most cases, those have been exhausted. It is an appeal to conscience. They have been on the road to redemption. Shouldn't society be as well?

First Encounters

From left to right, Sister Marie Elisabeth, Sister Pia Maria, Sister Mary Alix, Sister Lydia Maria, Sister Eva Nella

A Knock on the Door

GATESVILLE, TEXAS, is a prison town, a hundred miles north of Austin, with five of its six correctional facilities designated for female inmates. As you drive past the widely spaced campuses, surrounded by towering fences topped with coils of razor wire, you will notice women in white mowing the grass or edging the curbs. Mercury lights surround the perimeter of each facility and guard towers mark the corners. Before the land swells into gentle hills it stretches out into grassy pastures that, in the spring, fill with wildflowers rarely seen by the residents. On a nice day you might hear the correction officers taking target practice.

Set on a hundred acres off Farm to Market Road 215 is a low-slung single-story redbrick complex called the Patrick L. O'Daniel Unit. In the fall of 2014, Ronnie Lastovica, a Catholic deacon, was at the prison to assist in a Mass for the general population. Afterward, an officer told him, "There's an offender on death row who would like to take communion."

2024 was a turbulent time for women on the row; the state had just executed Lisa Coleman, the sixth woman to be killed in Texas since the U.S. Supreme Court reinstated the death penalty in 1976. Coleman was convicted of starving to death her girlfriend's nine-year-old developmentally disabled son, Davontae Marcel Williams.

Paramedics found his corpse in the women's apartment. He had 250 scars and weighed thirty-five pounds when he died. Davontae's mother accepted a deal and got a life sentence.

The officer conducted Deacon Ronnie to a building designated for crisis management. In addition to the condemned women housed in the unit there are additional cells where suicidal or mentally ill inmates are kept for observation. Barred doors on either side of a reception area called the Command Station lead to the two wings housing the condemned women. Above each door is the surprisingly voguish logo:

D
E
R A
O T
W H

A prisoner named Linda Carty was brought into a common room, which was painted bleakly white like everything in the unit, with four round tables and chairs bolted to the floor. Her hair, black with streaks of gray, was sternly pulled back in a ponytail. Her eyes were sometimes merry and sometimes sly. She was fifty-six years old and had been on the row for twelve years.

Linda was convicted of stealing a newborn baby and murdering the mother in the process; however, she has always maintained her innocence. Like the preponderance of those condemned in Texas, Linda was Black and poor. Born in the West Indies, she is a citizen of the British Commonwealth and entitled to assistance from the British consulate. Neither the prosecutors nor her attorney had advised her of this. After her conviction, the British government, which opposes capital punishment, belatedly hired the esteemed Houston firm Baker Botts to handle her appeals. They failed, and her case reverted to the Harris County district attorney to seek an execution date, which could come at any time. At that point, the only restraint is the DA's personal agenda. Texas prides itself on being a "tough on crime" state, and one powerful measure of a prosecutor's toughness is the number of people executed on their watch. The same goes for judges in Texas, who are elected. By itself, Harris County, the third most populous county in the United States, has executed more people than any other state, which is how it acquired the moniker of being the "capital of capital punishment." Thanks to skillful legislating on the part of death penalty advocates, the state has sanded down legal impediments that obstruct the road to execution in other states. As soon as the district attorney signs the death warrant, it goes to the judge in the jurisdiction where the conviction was obtained to set a date for the execution.

Deacon Ronnie and Linda recited the Penitential Rite—"I have greatly sinned"—then he offered her communion. They spoke for about an hour. Thereafter he visited her each week. Linda was outgoing and occasionally exuberant, boasting of breaks in her case that were coming her way but never actually arrived. "I'm going home," she would say. Ronnie didn't argue, but he also didn't encourage fantasies. "We have to be honest with our expectations of this place," he told me. He was not her lawyer. His assignment was to help her live until she had to die.

In February 2015, Linda mentioned to Deacon Ronnie that another woman would like to meet with him. "Tell me about her," he said.

Melissa Lucio, the only Hispanic on the row, was born in Lubbock in 1968, but after her father died, when Melissa was still an infant, the family moved to Harlingen, in South Texas, where her mother grew up. When Ronnie met her, she was housed in the wing of death row reserved for "non-work-capable" inmates. Those were women who broke rules or refused the opportunity to do the crafts that the prison provided and offered for sale. A prisoner may be moved to keep the peace within this group of violent offenders. The wing also offered an unofficial refuge for individuals who needed time alone. Like Linda, Melissa was near the end of her legal journey. She had been convicted of murdering her two-year-old daughter, Mariah Alvarez, one of her twelve children at the time.

Initially Deacon Ronnie was not allowed to see Melissa in the common room, so he met her outside her cell. All the cells are small—fourteen by six feet—"about the size of a parking spot at H-E-B," he said, naming a popular Texas grocery chain. Each cell has a barred window, coated in a film that has yellowed over time and casts a dim golden glow.

Melissa stood behind a barred door covered by a wire grate fine enough that only fingertips could touch from opposite sides. Her hair was shoulder length, with bangs—a black helmet framing a full face. She appeared totally defeated, her downcast brown eyes reflecting years of drug abuse, battering, and periods of homelessness. Her story echoed many Ronnie would hear. She was molested by various family members as a young child; married at sixteen, her husband abused her, as did other men she associated with. Her life was impoverished and full of violence. She sought escape in cocaine. A psychological expert who examined her said she met the criteria for many trauma-induced disorders, including depression, panic, and obsessive compulsion.

The deacon's ministry expanded. "One became two and two became three," Ronnie recalled. The next woman to be included was Brittany Holberg. A former sex worker, she had murdered an eighty-year-old man in Amarillo. Like Melissa, her life was a tale of abuse and addiction and the absence of stable relationships. Brittany was soon followed by Darlie Routier, convicted of killing two of her children and then staging an attack on herself, which included cutting her own throat. What set Darlie apart from most of the other women was that she had grown up middle-class, without poverty, drugs, and the cascade of abuse that shaped the narratives of the other women.

Then came Kimberly Cargill; she had set her intellectually disabled babysitter on fire. She had what appeared to be a pleasant childhood, cheerleading and performing on dance teams in high school, going to church camps in East Texas, and summering with her grandparents on a farm in Mississippi. She went on ski trips with Young Life, a Christian youth movement. She loved being around animals and gathering eggs early in the morning. Mental illness played a starring role in the tragedy of her life and that of other family members. "The cover of the book was different from the story in the inside sadly," she observed.

Finally, there was Erica Sheppard, who had, in the process of stealing a Houston woman's car, assisted in her murder. This was when Erica was nineteen. She is Black, and she has been on the row for three decades. She had hoped to become a nurse, but severe physical and sexual assaults damaged her brain. She saw her life as a constant search for safety.

Each of the women had been sentenced to death, but until that day came they were condemned to live with each other. They didn't know how. "They were like feral cats," Deacon Ronnie assessed. He now had six of them in his ministry.

A wild and improbable thought occurred to him.

East of Gatesville, in a suburb of Waco, behind a privacy fence of artificial brick panels, there is a convent of contemplative nuns called the Sisters of Mary Morning Star. A drainage ditch runs along one side of the property, attended by regal white egrets and black grackles striking ludicrous poses. Nearby are a few scattered office buildings, an Italian restaurant, and a major highway. It's not like some Old World monastery on a craggy mountaintop. It's a suburban ranch house in Waco.

Deacon Ronnie knocked on the door and presently a nun appeared, Sister Pia Maria, who had door duty. As contemplatives, the Sisters of Mary Morning Star don't teach or do missionary work; they spend their days almost entirely in silence, work, and study. They offer visiting hours, between two and five p.m.; a knock on the door is infrequent but not unheard-of.

Sister Pia Maria guided Deacon Ronnie into a little front room with a small wooden table and four uncomfortable chairs. Waiting there was the prioress, Sister Lydia Maria, a Mexican national whom Ronnie later described as a "fireball" and "quite the gal." She wore a gray habit that reached to her ankles and a white veil. The Sisters of Mary Morning Star add a matching gray scapular that drapes over the habit, which does a thorough job of erasing any physical features but heightens the drama of their faces. Sister Lydia Maria's face is alert, with keen features and piercing black eyes, owl-like in intensity.

Ronnie described his ministry in the six prisons in Gatesville, which included three thousand men and nine thousand women. "Then I dropped the shoe," he recalled. He proposed that the nuns visit the women on death row.

Sister Lydia Maria's eyes "got really big," Ronnie told me. "We don't go to prisons," she said firmly, although she offered to pray for the women and kindly asked their names. Prayer was what the order was created to do. Ronnie refused to take the hint; he continued to expound upon what a great idea it was. "We don't go out much," Sister Lydia Maria interjected, but Ronnie kept talking. He spoke about the condemned women, how they were struggling spiritually, but as a man there was a limit to the guidance he could offer. He pointed out that the nuns lived very similar lives—by choice. What could be more perfect?

Sister Lydia said the decision wasn't hers, she would have to ask permission of the order's leadership to do such a thing, but it was highly unlikely they would allow contemplative nuns to traipse off to death row.

"I know, I know, but would you pray on it?" Ronnie asked as he was finally escorted to the door.

They prayed. They deliberated, which was unusual in a vocation where silence was the rule. They were a brand-new order, and their boundaries were elastic and untested. Although they were silent, they hadn't taken a vow of silence. They were contemplatives but they hadn't entirely shut the door on the outside world like Carmelites. They consulted with their vicar, who was then in Wisconsin, Sister Mary Thomas. A cheerful product of Catholic schools and Notre Dame, she mulled over this startling challenge. On the one hand, going to the prison could set an unwelcome precedent. What did it mean to be a contemplative order if instead of spending the day in silence and prayer you are ministering in prison? And why *these* condemned women? The world is full of misery. Where would it end? On the other hand, the vicar believed in "providential encounters," such as the serendipitous knock on the door from Deacon Ronnie. "I'm very edified by him," Sister Mary Thomas told me. "He's a holy man. He makes the walls fall to serve these women." She consulted with Sister Lydia Maria and the women in the convent. Each of them was at once frightened by the idea but also compelled to respond to Ronnie's plea. Sister Mary Thomas told him, "Okay, we'll do it. We will meet these ladies and discuss our way of life—just this one time. If it helps them, that's wonderful. But that's all this will be, nothing else."

Ronnie

RONNIE LASTOVICA IS a cattleman. Slender and swaybacked, his face is pinched and narrow, mottled from the Texas sun, with a strong jaw and a small mouth marked by a crooked smile. He wears silver wire-rim glasses, although he's blind in his left eye, because of a detached retina, which is only detectable by the slightly larger pupil. I hadn't noticed it, but the ladies on the row, who scrutinize every detail of Deacon Ronnie, were quick to spot it. Despite his provincial background he doesn't drawl when he speaks, but it is the sound of a native, and he certainly talks a lot when he has a point to make. Verbally he will lasso you to a chair until you surrender to his whims, as happened to the Sisters of Mary Morning Star.

The Lastovica clan arrived in America in the person of Ronnie's great-grandfather, who landed at Galveston in the late 1800s and became a peanut farmer in Central Texas, one of the many Czech immigrants to populate the state. Ronnie's father, Clarence, ran a herd of Black Angus near Belton. Clarence died of congestive heart failure in 1992, when he was fifty-nine. The following Sunday, Ronnie's grandfather passed away. "Within seven days, I lost the two most powerful men in my life," Ronnie recalls. From then on, women would fill his emotional space. His mother, Marlene, taught elementary school for thirty-three years. She is eighty-eight, lives alone on the ranch, and still maintains a small herd of cattle, which Ronnie dismisses as "yard art." Father Harry Dean, a priest who worked in the prisons with Ronnie, observed, "Ronnie is his mother's son. She's a nice, generous, very Catholic woman, but she's tough. If he's a bulldog, she's Godzilla."

Ronnie grew up playing high school football on Friday nights and baseball in the summer. Work on the ranch was constant and never-ending. His first exposure to crime and punishment was on a Cub Scout field trip to the jail in nearby Temple. They weren't shown any prisoners, just an empty cell, but it made an impression. "I just remember being scared to death," Ronnie recalls. " 'Get me outta here!' kind of thing." He met his wife, Krissie, at Texas A&M, where he was class president in 1979. He studied agricultural economics on an army scholarship. He had never been on an airplane until the army flew ROTC cadets to Fort Riley, Kansas, for summer training. A few years later he was piloting Chinook helicopters in the Egyptian desert, as part of a NATO exercise.

Army life didn't satisfy him. He briefly attended law school. He bought a livestock auction barn with his brother and made a success. He and Krissie renovated a historic gingerbread house on Main Street in Belton, built by Ele Baggett, one of the legendary cattle drovers of the Chisholm Trail, which ran through town, down this very street. "On his last drive he took three thousand steers to Chief Red Cloud," Ronnie told me. He and Krissie raised a family, and Ronnie made sure the children learned how to ride and shoot.

Belton is the seat of Bell County, graced with a majestic courthouse on the square and the hardly surprising Confederate statue in front. It's a quiet town, belying the history of saloons and bordellos that huddled near the courthouse in the days of the Old West, when Belton stood at the edge of the frontier. In the late nineteenth century, a group of women started a religious collective formally known as the Belton Woman's Commonwealth but casually called the Sanctified Sisters. Beginning as a Bible study group, it caught on among women fleeing abusive marriages. They supported themselves cleaning houses, selling grocery staples, and making dresses, hats, shoes, and crafts. One of their members became a doctor and another a dentist. Wise investors, the Sanctified Sisters eventually purchased two hotels and a considerable amount of farmland. They raised money for the Elgin Opera House and established the town's first library. "Be good and be celibate" was their motto.

Men were permitted to live with the sisters if they adhered to the guidelines, but when two men associated themselves with the movement, they were kidnapped and beaten, then sent to the insane asylum in Austin.

An exhibit in the Bell County Museum quotes a passage from a historical study titled "The Sanctificationists of Belton":

> One night in the 1870s, a posse of disgruntled husbands demanded to see their wives, and at least one shot was fired at the house, which still scars the front door.
>
> It is said that the shot was only calculated to scare the women, as it likely did. But, having stood up to the withering scorn of the rest of the town, to previous threats of husbands and fathers, and to the heartbreak of severing family ties, a wildly aimed bullet that entered near the door hinge, hit the cornice in the hall and ricocheted, was not likely to break up the band. And it did not.

That said, in 1808 the Sanctified Sisters moved to a suburb of Washington, D.C. They became active in the women's suffrage movement. Their founder, Martha McWhirter, wrote to Susan B. Anthony, inviting her to join the sanctified movement. Anthony declined. "I cannot get my head into anything that is specifically woman's. I only want to have her made equal with man in this republic."

The movement died a slow death, along with the aging membership. The last member passed away in 1983, at age 101. The Sanctified Sisters would be remembered for creating the first women's shelter in the nation, one designed as a residential refuge for abused and abandoned women, in place of the asylums and reformatories and homes for unwed mothers that preceded the women's shelters of modern times.

Race and religion divide the town between the mostly White Southern Baptists and the mostly Hispanic Catholics. "We think everybody is going to hell if they're not one of us," Father Harry observed. "And yet they figured out a way to have a community and let their kids go to public high school." For decades nearly all the rampaging growth in Texas has taken place in the cities and allied suburbs, while little towns have been left to wither, but Belton has managed to slowly grow, in part because of nearby Fort Hood, the largest U.S. military installation in the world.

With a population of 23,000, Belton is still a place where you regularly run into everyone you know, but in Father Harry's opinion the community has become more estranged, along with the rest of America. "I see a lot more demonstrative presence of what I call super rednecks," he said. "They walk around with pistols in their butt cracks at 7-Eleven. They have Trump flags all over the place. When we were in Covid, they were resistors to vaccines."

One day in 1994, someone left a pamphlet on Ronnie's windshield describing the duties of a Catholic deacon. A note said, "You may have a calling for this." In the hierarchy of the Catholic Church, deacons are members of the clergy below priests, typically retired men looking to do some meaningful volunteer work, but Ronnie was thirty-eight years old, growing his business, and rearing a young family. "It certainly wasn't on my schedule." The idea took hold nonetheless and in June of 2000 he was ordained.

The following year, Ronnie was asked to check on four young men who had just been arrested in Bell County. It turned out these men had murdered two college kids. "That was my introduction to the prison ministry." The killers had dropped out of school and were roaming the streets. "These guys were just starving for some identity and to be loved," Ronnie says. They found it in organized crime. They each wound up with two forty-year sentences, "stacked," meaning they have to serve them sequentially, so they'll die in prison. One of them went through a ministry program in the prison, and Ronnie corresponds with him.

Ronnie ordered a clerical collar and a black shirt. When he first looked in the mirror he experienced an identity shock, such as one might experience when suddenly cloaked in a uniform of authority—or when reduced to the rough white tunic and baggy trousers of women prisoners in Texas. In 2014, Ronnie got a call from the Diocese of Austin asking him to include in his ministry the vast Gatesville prison complex. "It's just a bunch of women," he was assured.

Sisterhood

Over the last half century the number of nuns in America has dropped 80%, to 36,000, and the average age of a Catholic nun is 80. By contrast the Sisters of Mary Morning Star are young—the average age is 37. They split off from the Community of Saint John, in France, in part because they felt that it was overly controlled by meddlesome priests. After years of internal strife, Pope Francis allowed the breakaway nuns to start a new order, headquartered in San Sebastián, Spain. That was in 2014, the same year that Deacon Ronnie first visited death row. Since then, the order has grown to three hundred nuns in thirty convents around the world, empowered by the knowledge that if there is to be a future for Catholicism, a modern and expansive religious order must be a part of it.

At the convent near Waco, the nuns wake each morning around four forty-five and spend two or three hours praying together and chanting from "The Liturgy of the Hours," also known as the Divine Office, a paperback of some seven hundred pages of prayers, psalms, hymns, scripture, canticles, and chants that evolved from early monastic communities. This is followed by solitary Bible study and contemplation.

Each daily event is marked by a bell chime, an ancient monastic tradition. At six a.m. the nuns gather in the chapel for prayer and thirty minutes of hymns. Breakfast is at seven thirty. At eight thirty the first class begins, usually philosophy or theology. After more classes and prayer, the nuns convene in the kitchen to peel vegetables. Silently. Around noon there is more prayer, followed by Mass, more prayer, then lunch. All meals are eaten alone in their rooms, except Sunday lunch, when the sisters eat together but don't speak.

At two p.m., work begins—mainly, washing, cleaning, and crafts. The sisters are encouraged to develop a personal craft, such as leatherwork, calligraphy, embroidery, or making rosaries, soap, candles, or icons. They sell these products to support their convent. One sister arrived with a guitar, which she was going to give away, as it violated the sanctity that silence imposed, but the nuns decided that music was different from speech, and so the guitar remained.

At three the bell rings again, signaling prayer time to commemorate Jesus. Vespers at five thirty. At six there is Eucharistic adoration in the chapel. The Eucharist references the bread and wine that Jesus served at the Last Supper, telling his disciples, "This is my body" and "This is my blood." In the Catholic tradition, the Eucharist is not a symbol; through divine mystery it is literally the body and blood of Christ. Some of the nuns prostrate themselves while they pray before the Eucharist.

At seven p.m., the bell announces dinner, which is eaten alone. Evenings are free but short. The sisters may go for a walk, or pray, or read the Bible. They can talk, they say, but "We try to avoid it." Once a week there is recreation—walking, bicycling, soccer, basketball, or swimming—all accomplished while wearing habits, even in the pool. Occasionally there is a movie, but it's always about the life of a saint.

It's not as if the nuns of Mary Morning Star had tuned out the world. They have a house phone, and the prioress can give them permission to communicate with their friends and families. They live on a diminished diet of news, but they know who is president or what wars are under way. A key source of information about the world is the prayer requests from local parishioners or from Morning Star sisters across the globe—a kind of prayer hotline. Before the nuns met the women on death row, they were already praying for them.

The condemned women also awaken early, around four or five. "I start by putting water in my hot pot to make coffee, and while the water's getting hot, I make my bed, wash my face, and get dressed for work," Melissa Lucio told me. "We work from six thirty to ten thirty. So what we do is special projects in the work room. We crochet, we do embroidery and cross stitching." Darlie Routier, convicted of killing two of her children, makes stuffed animals—pigs, rabbits, dinosaurs. The women also make baby blankets. These items either go to Huntsville to be sold to state employees or are given to the corrections officers who guard them. The women normally eat in their cells, but they gather to celebrate holidays and birthdays. Darlie and Melissa are the "cooks." That means taking the prison-supplied meal and doctoring it with condiments and cheeses purchased from the commissary. Cut-up chicken, crushed potato chips, ranch dressing, cream cheese, and jalapeños approximate a high-calorie enchilada. Some of the regular food is so bad the officers apologize when serving it. (Prison officials deny this.)

Like the nuns, the condemned women spend their free time in their cells. Digital tablets now allow them to watch movies, which can be rented for thirty days, or call people on an approved list. "Those of us who have been here for so many years see it as a blessing," Brittany Holberg told me. "For twenty-five years all we were allowed to do was make a five-minute phone call, every ninety days, while handcuffed."

Television is the prison pacifier, but on death row the viewing hours in the community room are restricted and the women must agree on what to watch. Kimberly Cargill is a sports fan, and over the years various wardens have allowed the women to watch the Dallas Cowboys games, but in truth most of them weren't interested. They prefer cop shows. "I live on death row," Kimberly complained. "Crime is all around me. I mean, it was *FBI, Law & Order* . . . It just wasn't the mental break I cared for." She was overruled.

Despite there being only six women on death row when the nuns first visited (a seventh, Taylor Parker, arrived in 2022), Ronnie observed that there were cliques and hard feelings among them, which made prison life more miserable than it had to be. He noticed in other wards that female prisoners needed community in a way the men did not. Women create new family units, replicating nuclear families that they may not have enjoyed in their lives outside. Yet, because the condemned women inhabited a place of spiritual darkness, they fell into spats and backbiting. Emotional wounds were hard to heal. Some of the women were more isolated than others, but each of them suffered from the same cruel sentence—not just death but living with one another. If they were a family, they were a broken one.

Four nuns arrived at the O'Daniel Unit the evening of December 2, 2021, only two months after Deacon Ronnie's visit to their convent. He was waiting in the parking lot as they arrived. "They were so nervous, they were just shaking," Ronnie said. "They looked like little ducks walking."

Prison officers were prepared for the visit, but some were disquieted by the sight of the nuns, who represented an alternative authority. Ronnie observed of the guards, "They didn't want to misbehave or say something out of line. The whole place had this surreal sense of reverence when the nuns walked in." The sisters had to pass through a sally port, the double gate that opens to the no-man's-land between the perimeter fences, then they were

The Patrick L. O'Daniel Unit of the Texas Department of Criminal Justice, which houses death row, in Gatesville, Texas

escorted into the security office, where they presented their driver's licenses, which bore their secular birth names, not the names they were given by the order. Having taken a vow of poverty, they owned virtually nothing, so there was little to scan except the beaded rosaries that looped around their belts and dangled to their knees. They walked across a lawn into the unit as prison officers stared, then through another barred gate.

"To get to death row, you have to first pass through the psychiatric corridor, where the senses of smell and hearing are tormented with screams and repulsive smells," Sister Lydia Maria recalled of that initial visit. "We were approaching our destination and did not know what to expect." They passed the empty cells on death row, then an officer opened a door and the nuns in their gray habits entered the colorless community room, where the women in white were waiting. It was like walking into a black-and-white movie.

Deacon Ronnie said a few words of introduction. "Then something supernatural happened," Brittany Holberg recalled. "It was just instant. There was not a moment of discomfort. There was not a moment of unease. We opened our arms and they opened their eyes, and we embraced one another."

Neither group had a plan about how to proceed, nor did Deacon Ronnie, so the sisters began talking about their lives of contemplation and community life. They described what would be an ordinary day in the convent. The fact that they had so much in common came as a surprise to both groups. The women on the row were astonished that the nuns had *chosen* to live a life nearly as confined as their own, in rooms they, too, called cells. "We talked about having a corner," Brittany said. "I have a corner in my cell. That is where I pray and spend time with God. And they explained that they have their own sanctuaries in their cells as well." Sister Lydia Maria privately noted another commonality: "We are not beautiful women as the world would call us. We wear the same clothes. The women on the row cannot be afraid of us. They cannot feel lower than us. There's nothing in our appearance to make them feel not beautiful or not elegant."

A mysterious sorting process took place as the women sensed their ideal opposite. Kimberly Cargill immediately identified with Sister Pia Maria. "She's the one with the round face, like me," Kimberly said. They had both been nurses in their previous lives. "She was a bit teary-eyed," Sister Pia Maria recalled of their first encounter. "She was okay shortly afterwards and we bonded well. We laughed so much. . . . Since then, she calls me her giggle buddy."

Darlie Routier, who wasn't raised particularly religious, was baptized in prison into the Catholic Church in 2021—largely because of Deacon Ronnie's influence—and she had never spent any time with nuns. "I was thinking they were more stiff and rigid, and they were not like that at all," she said. "They weren't always nuns, some of them had careers. They still struggle with things like we all do daily." She added, "It was like we had known them all our lives. There was no hesitation. We all hugged and immediately started talking."

Melissa Lucio grew up Catholic but had never met a nun. The fact that the nuns had overcome their own "trials and tribulations" gave Melissa hope. "I get peace from them," she said. "I'm a new creation today. I'm not the same woman that I used to be."

Brittany was drawn to Sister Lydia Maria. "She was the first to say, 'You and I are very much alike,'" Brittany told me. "And my response was, well, I doubt that. That's when she began to share with me some of the things in her life, when she had been seeking something more and was doing things that were reckless—that took her to the edge—and realizing the emptiness that was found there. On that we greatly related, because I was able to share all the things that I was trying to find in my own life. I could not reach the place that I wanted to be. I found all of that when I surrendered everything to Him. And that's exactly what she had done." It wasn't a surprise to Ronnie that Brittany and Sister Lydia Maria discovered each other; he envisioned each of them as leaders in their community.

As the nuns retraced their steps through death row, they passed Erica Sheppard in her cell. She had converted to Islam eighteen years before and decided to skip the Catholic ceremony, but the nuns stopped and asked her name and said they were praying for her. "She gave us a big smile," Sister Lydia recalled. At the time, Erica had no teeth.

Once outside, the nuns told Ronnie, "We came here so afraid, and thinking we were going to minister to these women. And oh my goodness, they ministered to *us*." Tearing up in recollection, Ronnie told me, "It was the most captivating moment I've ever had."

The Whiskey Priest

Ronnie Lastovica was a man among many women, but for years his only real confidant was Father Harry Dean Jr. Before entering the priesthood Father Harry was a television journalist of the ambulance-chasing variety out of Odessa. He witnessed a lot of violence, which can take a toll, even on a world-weary reporter. He started drinking excessively, a lifelong problem, even after he turned hard to religion and became a priest.

Harry met Ronnie and Krissie when he was the pastor at Christ the King, their church in Belton, and they became close. The Lastovicas supported Father Harry through his alcoholism and rehab, and when he became sober he joined the prison ministry with Deacon Ronnie. Harry's title was vicar of priests, which nominally put him above Ronnie in authority, but Ronnie led the way. Indeed, it was physically hard to keep up with him. "He'd set the day where we do one unit after another unit after another unit, no break," Father Harry recalls. "Ronnie walks really fast. There's one speed for his gait, and it's haul ass. He was so super focused on what he had set to accomplish that day, he was just oblivious of everything around." As draining as this routine was, there were moments of redemption that Harry never thought possible. "I wouldn't classify Ronnie as a great communicator, except when God wants to use him, and then, brother, does he get the job done."

Father Harry, "The Whiskey Priest"

The despair of the inmates was endless and profound, and Harry's traumas were reignited by the suffering he witnessed. He and Ronnie would decompress at night as they drove the forty-five minutes back to Belton. Ronnie used the time to mentor Harry in the ministry they had chosen. "Look, you'll never get the full story," Ronnie told him. "Eventually, you'll get most of the story, as they begin to trust you and realize you're not there to harm them. These women have been abused so horribly they have to scan anybody who comes close to them. Once they understand that you're not a threat to them, they'll start unpacking."

Harry found his experience as a journalist to be useful when confronting the prisoners who dodged responsibility for their crimes. "I'm not going to say in the middle of confession, 'Hey, I read your trial transcript and you're not telling me the truth,' but I did use my training to throw prompting questions in front of them that might help them breadcrumb their way to actually coughing it up." However, the never-ending horror stories that were the daily diet wore Harry down. One night he was in the parking lot waiting for Ronnie to finish, looking at the stars, when he heard a sound so powerful it seemed to vibrate through the ground. It came from the psych ward. "Someone was mule-kicking the door and she was shrieking the whole time. I felt it in my body." He compared it to the shock of artillery practice at Fort Hood, which will shake the walls miles away. The odors were sometimes overpowering—the stench of feces, which the women on the psych ward would sometimes hurl at officers or visitors, and tear gas when behavior reeled out of control.

Harry concluded that it wasn't healthy to work in prisons all the time, constantly assaulted by waves of grief, anger, and hopelessness. "A guy should have a foot in parish ministry somehow," he explained to the church leadership when he sought to be relieved. "He needs to find a way to stay with polite people whose stories aren't all so ghastly. It really rattles your cage that this many people in our society have lived such screwed-up lives to the point they're so deformed. And yet, most of the citizenry of Texas doesn't give a flying shit about that."

Harry observed how the death row ministry had changed Ronnie. "His pragmatism took on a kind of enlightened creativity, enabling him to navigate the world of corrections management in a way to achieve ministry goals I wouldn't have thought achievable." At the same time, he saw how death row forced Ronnie to deal with the "ultimate expression of an unjust system." The friend he had known for years developed another side of his personality. "There's gentle, charitable, extremely kind, and self-giving Ronnie, and there's stubborn, my-way-or-the-highway Ronnie. When he's pissed-off, you're going to know it. He scared me sometimes." Harry had little patience with attitude problems and bad behavior on the part of the inmates. "I would come down hard," he recalls. "One time, the girls were just jacking around, not paying attention to the service," so Harry reprimanded them. "Ronnie turned and looked at me in the middle of the liturgy in front of all of them and said, 'Father, don't ever do that again.' "

"I knew he couldn't go out there and be effective and handle his business that way," Ronnie explains. "It was a charitable correction."

After six years, Father Harry walked away from the prison beat. He's still doing his best to handle the trauma he encountered there. Deacon Ronnie noted, "He's probably the only person in our diocese that has a clue about what I'm doing."

Father Harry's recollection reminded me of an unusually frank note Brittany sent me about the psych ward adjacent to the row. "As I write this the air around me is filled with shrieks and screams," she wrote. "The building I live in is titled 'crisis management' but many refer to it as the 'house of horrors.' Without a moment's notice chemical agents may be administered upon individuals who are refusing to comply with orders. Oftentimes my room is flooded with water that is filled with urine and feces. This has been my life for 28 years."

A Thought Experiment

Sister Lydia Maria

I WAS SURPRISED, in talking to the women on the row and to the nuns, that boredom was not a major issue—as it certainly would be for me—spending decades in a prison or a monastery with only a handful of other people. For the nuns, with their practice of prayer and contemplation, there is little opportunity for personal intimacy. The level of drama is severely diminished in such quiet surroundings, but so is the opportunity for genuine expressions of love, hate, curiosity, compassion—the entire arsenal of human feelings that open the gates of human understanding. The volatile women on the row are not handicapped by such restrictions, but they are also stuck with each other. Some are mentally ill or chronic liars. Some are submissive; others aggressive. Grudges develop; relationships freeze in place; years and even decades pass with little change, unless an execution date suddenly arrives that unites the women in restless anxiety.

"Your question cuts right to the heart of our contemplative life, with long moments of silence and solitude in order to confront this 'inner sanctuary' or 'chamber of the soul,' as Pascal put it," Sister Mary Thomas wrote me when I asked about boredom. "Spending long moments in the silence of prayer, a prayer of faith, is hard. It can be dry and sometimes feels useless. We don't always feel God's presence and consolation. It is both what attracts us and what is also the hardest. In thinking about my contemplative vocation and invitation to this life of silence in faith, I often jokingly sing to myself a line from the old U2 hit: *I can't live with or without you.*"

So it's not all prayer inside her consecrated brain; occasional Irish rockers intrude, but the focus always returns to prayer. Hour after hour, day after day, decade after decade. To me, it sounds deadly, but for Sister Mary Thomas it was the only career "radical" enough to contain her spiritual energy. "I can't live without this life of prayer," she said. "Even within the dryness or silence, there is a thirst in my heart that is fulfilled only by this contact with God. And if a day goes by without the time to be 'present to the one who is present to me' something is unsettled in me. The silence and solitude is all with a view—not to emptying my mind and being idle but to meeting a person, a person who can only be met when we stop to listen to the still, small voice in the depths of our inner chamber." That person is Jesus.

When the nuns first arrived in the prison, they knew nothing about the condemned women's crimes. It's also true that they knew very little about one another. The sisters live together, but they rarely speak, and the lives they left behind are seldom discussed. It's a kind of forced naïveté, in which gossip and news—

"useless chatter," in Sister Mary Thomas's evaluation—are pushed out of the mind, along with memories and moments of intimacy, by a regimen of continuous study and prayer.

I asked the sisters if they had ever experienced violence in their lives. They had not. The nuns and the condemned women had grown up in separate realities; one safe and predictable, the other violent and capricious; one that was buffered by love, the other that was cruel and degrading. It occurred to me that if a nun and a condemned woman were able to exchange their past lives, might the nun be on death row and the condemned woman in the convent? Sister Lydia Maria and Brittany immediately identified with each other; they are close in age, each bold and thoughtful, so I decided to compare their lives up to the moment they made a choice that would forever define them.

Sister Lydia Maria, with her intensely focused dark-chocolate eyes and expressive face, maintains an air of worldliness about her, like an actor playing the role of a nun. Engaged, amused, but also severe in her practice, one could imagine her as an executive in a multinational corporation; indeed, that was the direction she steered toward early in her career. She grew up in a Catholic family in Mexico, near the California border, the second of three daughters. Her actual birth name was Lydia Maria Mancilla Romero, so she didn't need to adopt a new religious name. "We had a happy childhood," she recalls. "I always felt loved and protected by my parents and my sisters." She attended Catholic school until she was fourteen, "but I had never wanted to be a sister—never, never—because I had a lot of energy, a lot of friends." Lydia loved travel, art, and music. She played the guitar. The idea of retreating to a convent and a life marked by silence was not the vibrant future she imagined for herself.

Had circumstances been different, Brittany might have been the more obvious candidate for the convent. She is physically striking, with green eyes and an inadvertently seductive manner. Like many deeply religious personalities, she teeters on the edge of ecstasy, besotted by the natural world and perpetually open to revelation. She composes meditations that she emails to her circle of supporters, written with an unexpected polish, given that she dropped out of high school and plunged into a world of depravity that only ended with her arrest for murder.

A native of Amarillo, Brittany was born addicted to heroin, due to her mother's drug habit. During much of her childhood, her biological father was incarcerated on drug charges. Another man, John Schwartz, a drug dealer, married her mother, Pamela, when Brittany was three, and adopted her a few years later. When Brittany speaks of her father, it is Schwartz she means. Her parents had a chaotic relationship, divorcing and marrying each other many times (Brittany remembers seven; court records say four) and living in a continual drug haze. As a child Brittany would sit in John's lap and pick the seeds out of his marijuana stash with her little fingers. At the age of four she was molested by a babysitter. By the time she was ten her parents were offering her drugs. Her mother would roll the joint for her.

Brittany was twelve when her favorite aunt, Karen Rose Murphy, was murdered. "She was the one person who always made me feel safe in the chaos of my parents' lifestyle," Brittany recalled. Now that pillar of stability was gone, shot to death by her husband. John Schwartz took Brittany to the morgue in Garland to identify his sister's body. The coroner told them they didn't want to see it, but he showed them a photo that has haunted Brittany ever since.

It fell to Brittany to clean up the murder scene in her aunt's apartment. John was incapable. "I remember scrubbing the blood-soaked carpet as my dad sobbed beside me and wishing he would go into the other room so he could not see," she told me. I imagine this young girl mopping up an ocean of blood, wringing towels in the sink, alone with the realization that this is what death is like, this is what awaits her. "I know all too well the grief that comes from such sudden and horrible loss," Brittany continued. "I watched it destroy my dad's family completely. I watched the anger eat them alive. I watched my grandfather drink himself to death and my grandmother turn into a shell of herself. And I watched my dad completely self-destruct." (Karen Murphy's husband, Vincent Murphy, was convicted of murder and sentenced to sixty years. He's not scheduled for release until 2047.)

In high school, Brittany volunteered as a candy-striper in a local hospital. "I would go from room to room and either fill water pitchers or just sit and talk with patients who seemed lonely or sad." The next summer she worked in the physical therapy ward. "I quickly figured out what the needs were and would just go to the patients who seemed scared or in the most pain."

When she was sixteen Brittany was working as a salesclerk at Chess King, a clothing store for teenage boys, in a local mall. She tried to keep up her studies but she was overwhelmed, dropping out of school in her junior year and getting her GED two weeks later. The director of the hospital where she had volunteered offered her a job as a technician when she turned seventeen. Brittany was thrilled. She was especially drawn to head-injury cases. "It amazed me," she told her defense attorney in an interview in 1997, after her arrest. "To see someone who was 'dead,' you know, they couldn't move, you could talk to them and they didn't hear you, in a coma, and then to watch them start to move and to walk was amazing." These transformations seemed like miracles. "I loved it," Brittany recalled. "It was like I was born to do it." She was finally on a path that might have led to a happy life, but there were dark forces ahead, pulling in the opposite direction.

Brittany recalled a moment from her critical teenage years. "I met a boy and we started to date," she told me. "He took me to his house, and there was a mother and a father and a brother and they were having dinner, sitting at a dinner table. And they watched a movie together. And I knew at this moment this was all I ever wanted." She added: "I didn't so much fall in love with the boy as I fell in love with the idea and ended up marrying the boy."

They were married on August 29, 1990, in Amarillo. Brittany was sixteen. That fall, her husband joined the military and left for basic training, and Brittany moved to Tulsa to live with his parents. There she taught aerobics at a women's gym. One day, right after Christmas, she was running in the woods along a creek when she was attacked by a stranger. Brittany was strong enough to break away and run back to the Holbergs' house. The description she gave of her attacker matched that of a man who had raped and murdered a woman recently. He began stalking Brittany and left messages in the mailbox. The police said they were afraid that the stalker would kill her if he had the chance; other than that warning, they had little to offer in the way of protection. At this point the army sent her husband home on leave to help Brittany pack up and leave Tulsa. She soon joined him at Fort Ord, an army base on Monterey Bay, California.

She explored the beaches and the rocky coastline. In the mornings she would walk out on the promontories as far as she could, then sit and watch the fog roll in, "like a giant white sheet spreading over the surface of the water," she wrote. "If it was quiet enough, I could hear the sounds those tiny particles of water were making along their journey, like the sound of Rice Krispies cereal when milk is poured over it. As it got closer, I would look out across Monterey Bay and take in all that my eyes could see, knowing that in a few moments I would be enveloped by the fog and everything else would disappear. In those moments there was a sense of peace."

Peace was what her marriage lacked. She and her husband fought constantly. Brittany informed him that when he graduated from basic training, she wanted a divorce, but she finally agreed to try to save their marriage. She lived with him for two years at the base, occupying herself by running the trails through the rolling grasslands above the Pacific. But that came to an end when she hyperextended her knee. A doctor on the base prescribed Percocet, an opioid. She was to take one pill every four hours. She doubled the dose. It wasn't a high; she just became numb. The doctor failed to monitor her increased usage, and if her husband paid any attention to the fact that his wife had become a drug addict, she didn't notice.

Then one day she threw the pills away. She didn't want to sink into that hole; she had seen what happened to her parents. Although she was sober, Brittany and her husband never settled into a comfortable marriage. That didn't change even when she became pregnant. She loved her baby girl but she also loved to party. Her marriage was dead. She didn't have a job. She had no direction in her life. She hated herself. And of course her parents were no help, but the following Christmas Brittany flew back to Amarillo to show off her baby. Once again she was drinking heavily.

Soon after she returned to the chaos of her family in Amarillo, she went to a dentist to attend to an abscessed tooth. The dentist gave her Vicodin, another opioid painkiller. This time she didn't throw the pills out. She saw how easy it was to take a prescription to a pharmacy and have it refilled. No one asked questions. A relative taught her how to forge prescriptions from dentists all over town. By now she was taking as many as a hundred pills a day. Her stepfather took her to rehab, but it was there she learned how to inject cocaine. She wound up in the hospital after being gang-raped, severely beaten, and stabbed.

In the hospital she considered who she was and how she had wound up in such a dismal spot. "I looked around at everything and thought: Maybe this is all I deserve," she recalled. "I was twenty years old. I had no education. I had a failed marriage. I spent a year and a half desperately trying to figure out how to make a life for myself and my daughter." Sex work provided an answer. She recalls thinking, "Maybe I'm too broken to have anything better."

During this period, the future Sister Lydia Maria was studying marketing at a college in Mexicali. She was still a believer but not so much a Catholic. Too many rules. She painted, she played basketball and tennis. "I was very alive. I had a boyfriend. I got a good job"—after graduation, she organized trade expositions—"but I wasn't a hundred percent happy." Life felt too safe for her. Although she was becoming a successful businesswoman with an ever-widening circle of friends, she began experimenting with extreme sports, such as skydiving and bungee jumping, but she was looking for something more than a thrill. Then, one day in March 2003, "I had a little accident."

She was on the freeway, driving too fast to work, and suddenly someone veered into her lane. Lydia turned sharply and her car went out of control. "So in these seconds that I was rolling over, I spoke with God. I said, *God, please, not yet. I still don't know what I was born for.*" She also prayed, "*Please don't let me hit and kill someone.*"

She was taken to a hospital. She had whiplash but no other injuries. But her perspective had changed. "I was more open to hear the voice of God." A year later, on August 14, she entered her religious vocation.

By this time, Brittany was on death row. It wasn't inevitable, nor was Lydia's decision to become a nun, but in each life there was a trajectory. No one rescued Brittany from the depravity of her family, and she wasn't strong enough to save herself. Her return to Amarillo was an act of surrender to the numbing bliss of the opioids. It was a suicide of personality. Brittany was still there physically, but a dark force had taken control.

If Lydia had been more seriously injured in the car wreck, she might have turned to painkillers to ease her suffering, as Brittany had, but she never sank into the trap of addiction. Her life was supported in so many ways that Brittany's was not. She was loved. She was safe.

Deacon Ronnie has counseled thousands of prisoners. The lesson he has drawn from that experience is the importance of family. Lydia's home life wasn't ideal; when she was fifteen her parents separated; the girls stayed with their mother, "but we always kept the bond with my father." Perhaps Lydia is just stronger by nature than Brittany, but who would she be if she had been born addicted, to parents who lured her into drugs? Who would Brittany be if she had been born into Lydia's good but not perfect family? The women on death row were all judged to have inflicted harm, and they are being punished for that. But aren't they also being punished for the traumas they suffered that in so many ways made them the people they are?

When I asked Sister Lydia Maria about this thought experiment, she responded through a theological lens: "If Brittany had had a beautiful family with love, protection, education, she would have had other opportunities, but I wonder, is it her painful experiences that have allowed her to be the woman thirsty and in love for God that she is today?"

Melissa

In 2017, a French American documentarian, Sabrina Van Tassel, came to the United States to interview women on death row. One of the few places that allowed such interactions was Texas. She found herself in Gatesville, talking to Melissa Lucio. Melissa had been convicted nine years earlier of killing her two-year-old daughter, Mariah. The medical examiner in Cameron County described bruises all over the child's body, and what she concluded were bite marks. "This wasn't an isolated incident where she lost it and she killed this child," the district attorney said at Melissa's trial. "She made this child *suffer*. Every time she injured this child she had to have gotten some pleasure from it because she didn't do it one time. She did it over a period of weeks and probably months."

"To tell you the truth, I didn't want to interview Melissa," Sabrina recalled. "Her story had sparked no interest from the media. It was nothing 'spectacular' or 'gruesome' enough, if you will. A very random case of child abuse." The "celebrities" on Texas's death row—the ones with the most heinous crimes—declined to talk, but Melissa agreed. Sabrina wondered, "What is there to say?"

Sabrina was a middle-aged Parisian woman, slender and confident, her hair worn in long brown tresses, her arched brows constantly signaling her emotions. Her smile is warm but sometimes countered by blazing eyes, which would clear many a path in her pursuit of Melissa's story. Before the prison interview, Sabrina visited Harlingen, a small town in the Rio Grande Valley near the border with Mexico. She began digging into Melissa's background, which resembled that of so many women convicted of violent crimes. Melissa had been sexually abused as a child. She married at sixteen and was abandoned by her first husband, with whom she had five children, and by her next, who fathered nine. She was chronically impoverished, sometimes homeless, and lost custody of various children. She had been a cocaine addict. There was little to suggest she was in any way redeemable, let alone innocent.

On February 17, 2007, paramedics arrived at the Lucio residence, in Cameron County, on the Mexican border, and found two-year-old Mariah unresponsive on the floor. When one of the responders, trying to resuscitate the child, took off Mariah's shirt, everyone noticed the bruises. Melissa explained that Mariah had fallen down the stairs two days earlier. The responder was immediately suspicious, because the Lucio residence was a single story. He alerted the police. In fact, the Lucio family had just moved into their new, nicer dwelling the day before, with only three steps at the front door—not fourteen, as in the previous apartment. Based on this fundamental misunderstanding, Melissa was taken into custody. Meanwhile, Mariah was declared dead in a local hospital. The medical examiner later said that little Mariah had suffered the worst case of abuse she had ever seen.

Sabrina interviewed members of Melissa's family. They said that Melissa had never abused any of her children at any time. Melissa had been cleaning houses for a living, and when Sabrina talked to people who employed her they all said Melissa wasn't capable of violence. She learned that Mariah, a toddler, was pigeon-toed and frequently tripped. One of Melissa's children told Sabrina that he had witnessed Mariah falling down the steep, rickety outdoor staircase, and several other children said that Mariah's health had declined abruptly in the two days after the fall. That information wasn't presented at the trial, so Sabrina filed an open-records request. She found evidence that the eyewitness testimony had been suppressed.

Sabrina also learned that, before the trial, Melissa's court-appointed attorney, Peter Gilman, had applied for a job in the district attorney's office, which he then joined right after the case concluded. Gilman's wife was already working for the judge. The district attorney who prosecuted her case, Armando Villalobos, was subsequently convicted of bribery, extortion, racketeering, and offering favorable treatment to members of a drug cartel, such as selling reduced sentences. He had arranged with a bondsman to get a kickback on the half-million-dollar bail posted by a convicted murderer, who he knew would flee custody. The murderer whose bail he arranged later killed again. Villalobos was sentenced to thirteen years and served six. Corruption had taken over Cameron County justice, and everyone knew it, but Melissa was too poor to offer the prosecutor anything but another notch in his belt.

Sabrina still wasn't convinced that Melissa's story was what she was looking for. She had confessed, after all.

Sabrina arrived at the prison in Gatesville in April 2017, after her trip to South Texas. She sat in the interview room, waiting for Melissa to be unshackled and strip-searched. The room is long and divided by plexiglass. On the visitor side there are framed jigsaw puzzles, a chalkboard, and a small library of children's books. Melissa entered and picked up the telephone receiver. She had never met a reporter before. For the occasion, her cellmates had put her hair in a bun and used a ballpoint pen for eyeliner. Sabrina asked about Mariah's accident and why Melissa hadn't sought medical attention for her after the fall. Melissa said she had just regained custody of her children a few months before and was worried that the county would permanently remove them.

Reporters strive to be objective, but instinct also plays a powerful role. Melissa came across as meek and sincere. It might be an act, but she seemed incapable of deception. There was none of the aggressive pretense or special pleading that might be expected of a duplicitous criminal. Sabrina was shaking as she left. "Time stopped," she said. She told Melissa, "We'll talk soon," then she turned to cameraman and said, "This is the next three years of my life." In the parking lot, Sabrina called Melissa's appellate attorney at the time, Margaret Schmucker. "I've just met your client," she said. "I want to know everything about this case." She added: "There's something really wrong." Schmucker responded, "I've known that Melissa was innocent for nine years now. We've been waiting for someone from the press to get interested." Unfortunately, she added, it was too late. Appeals were failing, one after another, and an execution date would soon be produced.

Melissa's confession and the medical examiner's gruesome report remained potent arguments for guilt. A video of Melissa's interrogation was shown at the trial. She was sitting in a chair in a small office, little more than a cubicle, in the Harlingen police station, next to a desk with a printer and a phone. She appears terrified and exhausted. The interrogation began around ten p.m. Four police officers loomed over her, taking turns as they pressed her to confess. She was given no food, though she hadn't eaten all day. She was in shock and mourning the death of her youngest child, and she was pregnant with twins.

"This is your chance to set it straight," one of the officers told her. "Because right now it looks like capital murder . . . Are you a cold-blooded killer or were you a frustrated mother who just took it out on her?" Melissa shook her head. She seemed to be in another world.

While the officers grilled Melissa, some of her older children were in another office denying abuse and corroborating their mother's story. A female officer asked one of her sons, "Did you see your sister fall down the stairs or did somebody tell you that she fell?" The boy replied, "No, I saw her fall."

Late that night Victor Escalon, a Texas Ranger, slipped into the office where Melissa was being questioned. In Texas, an aura of power and authority follows this elite state law-enforcement agency, which was founded in the early days of the Republic of Texas. Escalon wore the iconic white Stetson with the circular Ranger badge that is stamped out of a five-peso Mexican coin. Until that moment the interrogation had gone nowhere. The detectives took turns loudly accusing Melissa of being a bad mother and a depraved murderer, waving photos of Mariah's discolored corpse in front of her, but Melissa denied her guilt more than a hundred times. She had no counsel there to advocate for her.

The Ranger noticed that Melissa avoided eye contact and buried her head in her hands. "Right there and then, I knew she did something, and she was ashamed of what she did," he later testified. Her posture gave it away.

"Melissa," he said softly as he took over the questioning, "we already know what happened." The Ranger set his Stetson in the bookcase and pulled his chair closer, knee to knee. "Melissa, look at me," he said in his soft, commanding voice. Melissa looked at the face of this young officer, his hair closely trimmed, with his service weapon holstered on his belt. She was thirty-seven years old, submissive, wearing worn jeans and a plaid flannel shirt over a black T-shirt, her hair pulled into a ponytail, exhausted, overwhelmed, her eyeliner smeared from crying. "It happens, we all make mistakes," the Ranger said. He told her again, "We already know what happened." He said she would spend the rest of her life in prison. She wouldn't be able to see her children grow up and get married. Each of these threats proved absolutely true.

The passing hours made it clear that the questioning would not stop until she confessed. Confession would help her, Escalon promised. People will understand. He knew it was hard but it was the only way to find peace. At one point, Melissa said, "I don't know what you want me to say. I'm responsible for it." And then: "I guess I did it." The language was tentative, hypothetical, not the magic words Escalon and the other police officers who were participating in the interrogation were looking for. There was "just that little piece missing," Escalon said in court.

He produced a life-size baby doll in pink overalls. He set it on the desk then went into the hallway with the other officers, leaving a wilted Melissa alone with the doll. She propped her head on the desk, next to the baby doll, while the officers stood in the hallway. She could hear them talking about what to charge her with—injury to a child or "capital murder," a crime so severe that it can be punished with the death penalty. In Texas, this category includes killing a child under ten. This conversation was possibly staged to persuade Melissa to confess to a lesser charge.

"Today's date is June 18, 2007, it is three a.m., we are here at the Harlingen police department," Escalon said for the record when he returned to the room. It was time to close the deal. He set the baby doll in front of Melissa and said firmly, "What did you do?" He explained: "I want you to show us how you hit the baby."

Melissa put her fingers to her mouth, entranced, studying the doll. "I was combing her hair," she began. Gently, Escalon guided her into the act of spanking the doll. She complied. Escalon insisted she wasn't hitting the doll hard enough, demonstrating for Melissa how to hit with force. Her eyes were big and she smacked the doll repeatedly.

"What's going through your head?" Escalon asked.

"I wish it was me that got hurt, not her," she said, covering her face.

"It's three fifteen a.m., and that will end the interview."

It's hard to know how many people have been convicted of crimes based on false confessions, but about a third of those persons who have been exonerated by DNA evidence had falsely confessed to the crime. Given Melissa's lifelong history of abuse, the loss of a child only hours before, the sleep deprivation, and the experience of hours and hours of being in a small office at the mercy of five relentless interrogators, with no attorney at her side, the probability of a false confession was quite high. In that act of spanking the doll, Melissa signed her life away.

The forensic pathologist had been told before Mariah's autopsy that Melissa had already confessed, so she was predisposed to find evidence of a crime. The bruises were the result of abuse, she testified, as were the "bite marks" on the left arm and her upper back. One of the wounds was "a bite with raking, where it just pulls the flesh off the back." It sounded as if the child were being eaten. Such wounds could not be the result of falling down the stairs, the pathologist testified. Evidence of bite marks has been repeatedly shown to be scientifically invalid. In 2015, a Texas man who had been convicted based on bite-mark analysis was exonerated, and the Texas Forensic Science Commission recommended a moratorium on the use of such evidence.

Sabrina's documentary, *The State of Texas vs. Melissa,* premiered at the Tribeca Film Festival in 2020, after three years in the making, just as Sabrina predicted when she first met Melissa. The revelations did not sway the U.S. Court of Appeals for the Fifth Circuit—the last stop before the Supreme Court for inmates in Texas. The year before, in 2019, a three-judge panel of the Fifth Circuit had overturned Melissa's conviction, ruling that the evidence withheld violated her constitutional right to present a complete defense; but two years later, the full bench of Fifth Circuit judges—the conservative wing now enlarged by Trump appointees—overturned the ruling by a vote of 10–7, saying that Melissa's case did not merit a retrial or any other form of relief. Three of the judges who voted against her retrial admitted that the suppressed evidence—the eyewitness testimony of two of her children that Mariah had fallen down the stairs—might have cast doubt on the credibility of Melissa's confession. "That exclusion was the key evidentiary ruling at trial," the judges acknowledged.

The judges knew that Melissa's defense counsel was in the pocket of the prosecutor, who was a criminal, who was selling his office, and who believed he needed a death penalty conviction to boost his campaign for a congressional seat. Moreover, the evidence now showed that not only was Melissa innocent but that no actual crime had occurred. Nonetheless, the court was willing to let her die despite the likelihood she wouldn't have been convicted in a fair trial.

The Fifth Circuit sent the case back to the Texas Court of Criminal Appeals to weigh in, which rejected it, shutting the door on any other appeal. At that point, the state courts become eligible to set a date for execution, and the new district attorney in Cameron County swung into action. On January 20, 2022, he set the date and the clock began to tick. A fog of gloom settled over the row.

The Last Supper

THE CONDEMNED LIVE in the shadow of their execution, measuring their distance from the death chamber by the failure of their appeals. Most of the women on the row had court-appointed attorneys at trial, but after conviction a new set of lawyers often takes over. In Texas, the prisoners are represented by lawyers from the Office of Capital and Forensic Writs or paid appointed attorneys. Lawyers from the Federal Public Defender's Office typically represent the condemned in federal habeas appeals. The difference in expertise between the polished appellate representatives and the original trial attorneys is often shocking, which is one reason so many appeals cite incompetent representation. "When you get upstream with a death penalty case, you're going to get the best of the best," Deacon Ronnie observed. Assisting those appellate lawyers are wrongful-conviction specialists, such as the Innocence Project, which took on Darlie Routier's case after concluding she had a credible claim of innocence. A cadre of legal scholars with deep experience in death penalty cases and who know all the avenues of appeal can coach the lawyers as they wend their cases through the court system. "They'll try everything, procedural law, case law, whatever they can throw at it," says Ronnie. "It does buy time. It buys them a lot of time, actually." Erica Sheppard has been on death row for three decades. It can be very frustrating for the families and loved ones of the victims, who see execution as the only penalty worthy of the crime. On the other hand, standards change, new evidence arises; the drawn-out appeals allow for fresh eyes to assess the justice of the original conviction and sentence.

Despite the top-notch legal talent, and the almost universal procedural delays, it is formidably difficult to reverse a death penalty conviction, even where there is doubt of guilt, because of the institutional reluctance to question a jury verdict. Once appeals begin, the burden of proof shifts to the defendant. Instead of a reasonable doubt of guilt, the defense lawyers must demonstrate overwhelming evidence of innocence or constitutional violations. In Texas, when the appeals run out, the case lands back on the desk of the district attorney, who may then seek an execution date from a judge. At that point the machinery of death begins to move, and it moves swiftly.

In January 2022, Darlie, Erica, and Brittany met in the community room, where they found Melissa sobbing by herself. "We knew something was going on," Darlie remembers. "She finally got it out. They had given her a date. She said, 'I don't want to die.' And that just killed me. It was like being pierced in the heart. We all hugged her and talked to her. We just let her cry."

Melissa had ninety-seven days to live.

Krissie Lastovica was head of Adult Faith Formation and Religious Education at their local Catholic church in Belton. With curious eyes, a quick smile, her hair in a brown bob, she had the appealing quality of being both herself and an amused critic of herself. When she married Ronnie, in 1980, she envisioned life as an army wife, which would have been fine. Then he went to law school, and that was fine, too, although the law didn't hold him either. For the next twenty-nine years she was the wife of a successful cattleman.

Deacon Ronnie and Krissie Lastovica

But for the last two decades she found herself wed to a Catholic deacon whose career increasingly involved talking to the most dangerous people imaginable.

Ronnie had become ploddingly earnest in his singular mission, dazzled by the divine authority he assumed when he put on his clerical collar. Krissie sincerely honored his vocation, but it was a part of his life she knew about only glancingly. With each head-spinning shift in his life's direction their relationship endured—deepened, according to Ronnie—but he always shielded her from what actually went on in the prisons and the haunting stories that he was hearing. "Sin is horrible and my family didn't need the details," he decided. His silence left a lot of room for Krissie's imagination to fill in the blanks.

So she was stunned when Ronnie asked if she would come to the prison with him. The nuns were making their second visit, and Ronnie had conceived the notion of a farewell dinner for Melissa. She would be going into seclusion soon, thirty days before her execution. Ronnie thought Krissie would help a group meal go more smoothly; she had those social graces. But first he asked her to pick up his order at H-E-B and then swing by the church and make an urn of coffee.

Krissie had never been in a prison. Now here she was picking up party supplies for a celebration on death row. Typically, Ronnie had overordered—a deli plate, fresh sandwiches, relish tray, cheese tray, deviled eggs, the deluxe vegetable platter, the gourmet fruit tray, two huge cakes (frosted vanilla white cake and chocolate fudge), as well as the assorted chips and dips that the women had savored when they were at liberty to wander the world. Beverages included Dr Pepper, Sprite, and Hawaiian Punch. At the request of the women he even got fancy creamers for the Starbucks coffee Krissie brewed. "Free-world food is a big deal for them," Ronnie observed.

Half the coffee spilled in Krissie's backseat—an omen of what was to come, she feared. She sat in the prison parking lot staring at the guardhouse and the fences topped with coiled razor wire. Everything screamed danger. "My stomach, honestly, was just like: I don't know if I can do this." But when the sisters arrived in their van, Krissie introduced herself and admitted she was really nervous about meeting the inmates. "I have nothing in common with these ladies, I don't even know what I'm supposed to say or do," she told the nuns. They assured her they had felt the same way. Finally Ronnie showed up and escorted them all in, along with the mountain of food.

The condemned, in their cells, waved joyously at the nuns. "It was just surreal watching these women who were behind bars being so *happy*," Krissie told me. She spread white paper tablecloths and began setting out the food but when the inmates were let into the community room they obviously wanted to help, so Krissie turned things over to them.

The walls of the community room were decorated with paintings of birds, bits of scripture, and upbeat precepts, reminiscent of an elementary school classroom:

"Start each day with a grateful heart."

"Your only limit is your mind."

"Believe you can and you're halfway there."

"I can do all things through Christ, who strengthens me."

Krissie knew little about nuns or the condemned women other than the names Ronnie occasionally mentioned, which she began to match to their faces. She quickly discerned the family hierarchy that the women had created on the row. Erica and Melissa were obviously close. "They were the helpers," Krissie decided. "Brittany, she was more of a 'take charge, put this here, this is where this needs to go.' But the thing I thought was so wonderful was that every single one of them, when they had all this food on the table, would go and ask the others, 'Do you want any more? Can I get you this? Any more coffee?' I would have thought they would have been in it for themselves, like, 'I'm just gonna get my stuff and eat it.'" Although the women on the row were friendly, they asked Krissie unnervingly informed questions about the Lastovica children. "I kept thinking, Here is a whole set of people that know about my family. And if you get out, will you be coming to my house?"

Sister Mary Thomas, the vicar who had approved the sisters' first visit, had traveled from Wisconsin to witness the encounter. She was immediately impressed by the compassion of the prison officers. "The whole team was just very fraternal and kind and respectful," she said. There was a sense that the rules had softened in honor of Melissa, the meekest of them all.

Deacon Ronnie had a plan. He had orchestrated the encounters between the nuns and the condemned in order to teach the ladies on the row how to live with each other. When all the women had gathered in the room, he arranged them in a circle, nuns on one side, prisoners on the other, half in chairs and half sitting on the floor. Sister Mary Thomas spoke of a practice called the Chapters of Fault. "When we live in community, we inevitably hurt each other, out of laziness, selfishness, or pride," she said. "Too easily, tensions and misunderstandings can grow and make our community life unbearable." Weekly chapters were a way of harmonizing the group. Following Sister Mary Thomas's discourse, each of the sisters confessed their failures, apologized for slights, and gave thanks for little gestures that had been meaningful, demonstrating the humility required for communal living. These were lessons derived from monastic traditions across the millennia.

Suddenly Melissa spoke to her companions. "I just want to thank y'all for your love and kindness. You've been so good to me." She asked forgiveness for the ways in which she had been short with them. "It has been so hard, but your love and goodness give me so much strength." Her execution date was now forty-eight days away.

As other condemned women spoke, Krissie sat behind the circle, with Deacon Ronnie, quietly observing. "I didn't really feel a part of it," she said. One of the ladies asked to be forgiven for her impatience, which was not something Krissie would have thought required forgiveness, but then she recalled that these women lived together twenty-four hours a day, year after year, decade after decade, until death found them. "And that just blew my mind."

Krissie's thoughts were interrupted when it came to Brittany's turn. At home, Ronnie had spoken of her often; obviously there was a powerful connection between them. "I wanted to ask forgiveness of all of you," Brittany said. "I've been difficult and distant these last few days, but I love you all so much." Then she turned around and looked directly at Krissie. "I want to thank you for sharing your husband with us. You have no idea how much he has done for us—coming to see us twice a week, even during Covid when he would sometimes have to wait in his car for hours for the test to clear." She said, "He's been like a father to us."

Hanging over this event was the unstated parallel between the fate of the women and that of Jesus, who was also condemned, imprisoned, and executed. The nuns wondered if they would ever see Melissa again. This was effectively her Last Supper.

Death was a solemn guest in the room but joy was also present. One of the sisters brought a guitar and the nuns serenaded the ladies with liturgical songs; presently some of the prisoners pitched in with songs that were popular when they were young and free. Erica's deep, bold voice harked back to her youth in a Baptist church choir.

During the meal, Krissie sat at a table with Brittany and Sister Lydia Maria. Brittany was fifty now, but still girlish and buoyant, with a long face, arresting green eyes, a strong chin, and brown-blond hair now graying. She committed her crime when she was twenty-three, in 1996. Like some of the other women on the row, she longed for a role that would give purpose to the life she has left. When Sister Lydia remarked that the Sisters of Mary Morning Star maintain a convent in Ukraine, despite the war, Brittany brightened and said, "If I were free, I would go to Ukraine to help the sisters and to give hope to all the suffering victims of war."

Sister Pia Maria and Kimberly sat together—the giggle buddies—and Kimberly was surprised how enthusiastic Pia Maria was about the food. "She was *sooo* excited to eat that cake! She explained they do not get those things either. They had to get permission for the special treats."

At the end of the party, Deacon Ronnie led the communion and blessed the small congregation with holy water. He was astonished that all the food was gone. It could have fed half the prison. "Everybody was as full as a tick," he said, but he was still mystified by the prodigious consumption. "I know how they did it," Krissie recalled. Each of the ladies on the row came to the party wearing a jacket capacious enough to stuff with leftovers. Not a crumb remained.

Krissie realized this would be the last time she would see Melissa. "I didn't know what to say," she told me. "You can't say I'll see you later. You can't say nice to meet you, have a good life. What would you say? So I just looked at her and said, 'I have no words. I don't know what to say.' And she said, 'Don't worry about it, it will be okay.'"

The Uprising

Roll Call of the Executed

THE FIRST WOMAN legally put to death in Texas was Jane Elkins, an enslaved person, convicted in 1853 of using an ax to murder the slaveholder whose children she was caring for. Elkins had no attorney and, of course, no rights, facing an all-White male jury. Some historians believe she killed her enslaver after he raped her. No other motive was offered.

The next woman to be executed was Josefa "Chipita" Rodríguez, in 1863. She was convicted of robbing and murdering a horse trader who was carrying $600 in gold. When the gold was later found—in the Nueces River, near the victim's body—the motive became unclear. As with Jane Elkins, the murder weapon was an ax; like her, Chipita Rodríguez was tried without counsel. Chipita's only words in the courtroom were "Not guilty." The jury recommended mercy but the judge ordered her hanged the following day. (A century later, the Texas legislature exonerated Chipita because she did not receive a fair trial. The same has not happened with Jane Elkins.)

More than a hundred and thirty years passed before another woman was executed in the state, Karla Faye Tucker. Her crime, trial, prison experience, and execution each established a template for the women who would follow her to the execution chamber. During a robbery attempt, she and a male accomplice murdered an acquaintance, Jerry Lynn Dean, and a woman who happened to be in bed with him. Tucker and her accomplice snuck into the apartment intending to "case the joint" with the intention of stealing a motorcycle. They unexpectedly found Dean and his companion. Tucker happened upon a pickax, which Dean used in his work. She must have channeled some psychic tie to the ax killers who preceded her. She brought it down on Dean's head, slicing his eyeball in half. And then again, and again—twenty-eight times in total. She later said she got sexual release from the killing: "I come with every stroke." Then she turned to the woman who had pulled the covers over her head. Karla Faye struck her repeatedly and left the pickax buried in her heart. It wasn't hard for the prosecution to establish that she was guilty of the crime; she admitted it on a secret recording and couldn't help boasting about it.

In prison, Karla Faye found God. No one disputes the sincerity of her conversion. She was repentant. She was also attractive; with sparkling eyes and a vivacious, childlike spirit; there was something oddly angelic about her. In the minds of many conservative Christians, as well as the victims' families, she was redeemed, no longer the same person who killed their kin. She cast a spell over the entire prison system; officers and inmates alike were moved by her transformation. Eighteen prisoners offered to take her place on the gurney.

Her companions on death row saw her as a model. Erica Sheppard remembers Karla Faye as a great practical joker. Darlie Routier was assigned to work with her on special projects—commissioned works, such as dollhouses and knitted blankets. "I was very immature in my faith at the time and was struggling with a lot of my emotions," Darlie recalled. "Karla helped me deal with an inner battle I was going through for the hatred and the anger I had for who really did this to me and my boys."

A friend of mine, the writer Beverly Lowry, wrote a book about Karla Faye, *Crossed Over*. When they met, Beverly was still grieving her son, Peter, who was killed by a hit-and-run driver. At the time, Karla Faye wasn't giving interviews, despite the media frenzy that surrounded her crime and the novelty of executing a woman, but she found a soulmate in Beverly. Both Karla Faye and Beverly were a recognizable type of Texas woman, tough and clear-eyed, no-bullshit types. They became close. Beverly confided to Karla Faye the story of her son's death and the never-solved mystery of who had killed him.

"I want to ask you something," Karla Faye said through the plexiglass that separated them. "How would you feel if they found the driver of the truck that killed Peter and there was a trial and they brought the driver up and said, 'Oh, but he's changed, he's a new person now. See how good he is?' How would you feel?"

Beverly stumbled over the question, then admitted, "I don't know."

"That's why I don't give interviews," Karla Faye said. "It doesn't matter what I'm like now. I've done enough."

"Karla Faye Tucker put a face on the death penalty," Governor George W. Bush wrote in a campaign memoir, *A Charge to Keep*. He admitted that he was affected by her spirit. "At five three and 120 pounds, with wavy brown hair and large, expressive eyes, Karla Faye Tucker did not fit the public image of a typical death-row inmate." During his six years in the governor's mansion, Bush approved 152 executions. They became so routine people stopped noticing, or caring. Karla Faye changed that. It wasn't just Texas; people all over America and other countries felt an emotional prohibition toward killing a woman. The state had killed thirty-seven men the previous year, the most of any state since the death penalty was restored, with little outcry. Karla Faye changed that.

Pamela Perillo would serve forty years in Texas prisons, half of it on death row, before her sentence was commuted to life (she was paroled in 2019). She remembers the "media circus" surrounding Karla Faye. Ministers contended for her attention. Every day, boxes of mail from all over the world arrived, so much that Karla Faye couldn't answer it all. She asked her church to respond to some of the letters, and the church seized the opportunity to solicit donations. "I threw my Bible in the trash," Perillo recalls. "I wanted nothing to do with them. But I knew it wasn't God, it was man."

Within the small community of death row, the view was that Governor Bush had no choice but to proceed with the execution. "Texans used to think you should protect women, not kill them," Perillo observed. "But laws change and people change. It was time to kill a woman and Karla was the one." She adds: "It would have been political suicide for Bush not to execute Karla." Bush respected the fact that Karla acknowledged her guilt. "I know that justice and law demand my life for the two innocent lives I brutally murdered that night," she wrote to Bush and the Board of Pardons and Paroles. "I accept that." She explained that she used to blame her mother for shaping the person she became. "At 14 she took me to a place where there was all men and wanted to 'school me' in the art of being a call girl," she wrote. Karla Faye knew it was wrong, but she wanted to please her mother. She once blamed drugs, but now she held herself responsible. "Had I chosen not to do drugs, there would be two people still alive today. But I did choose to do drugs, and I did lose it, and two people are dead because of me." At the end of the letter, she requested that her sentence be commuted so that she could help others through her Christian ministry. "I can't bring back the lives I took," she conceded. "But I can, if I am allowed, help save lives. That is the only real restitution."

Bush's friends in the evangelical community were deeply opposed to executing her. "They felt Karla Faye Tucker was a living witness to the redeeming power of faith, and they were praying for her," Bush wrote. "I could feel their anguish." Pope John Paul II appealed to the governor to show mercy. One of the governor's own daughters announced at the dinner table her opposition to the death penalty. "It made my heart a little heavier," the governor recalled. "I explained to her the rationale for my support of the death penalty, that I believed the threat of being put to death might deter someone from taking another life."

Tucker's last meal was a peach, a banana, and a garden salad with ranch dressing. "She truly was not afraid of being executed," a prison official recalled, "she literally skipped down the hall to the death chamber, because she was convinced she was going to a better place." She was executed on February 3, 1998.

Since then, five other women have made the same journey to the death chamber in Huntsville, the heart of the Texas prison system. In 2000, there was Betty Lou Beets, known as the Black Widow for having killed at least two of her five husbands. Brittany Holberg had only just arrived on death row when Beets was executed. "I looked at this woman and I saw a grandmother," she recalls. "What possible threat to society could she be?" Frances Newton was next, in 2005. "She was like the sister I never had," Erica remembers. Kimberly McCarthy (not to be confused with Kimberly Cargill) had killed her neighbor during a robbery. "Kimmie came the same year as me and so she and I shared many years of life," Brittany recalls. "We were as close as two people can be." Melissa remembers Kimberly as a "loving, gentle woman, very supportive," who helped her with Bible studies. "We had a wonderful friendship." Erica remembered: "She loved to laugh, loved to cook, and she had so much peace when she got a date." She was executed in June 2013. Suzanne Basso, convicted of killing her boyfriend for insurance money, was severely handicapped and lasted only one day on death row before being placed in a medical unit, so the other women didn't get to know her before her execution in January 2014.

Lisa Coleman was the last woman Texas executed, in September 2014. During her time on death row, she and Darlie became very close. "I knew she didn't get a chance because she was Black," Darlie says. "She was poor. She was gay. She was a former gang member." Darlie was White and had lived a comfortable suburban existence. "She really challenged me because she showed me another side of life."

Darlie moved to the non-work-capable side of the row to be close to Lisa in her last month, then watched as Lisa was chained and taken from the row for the long drive to Huntsville. "I feel Lisa was at a place of peace when they killed her," Darlie says. "She knew where she was going." Lisa's final words on the gurney fondly mentioned "the girls on the row." She added: "Tell Darlie I love her."

The sentence of death in Texas is not a solitary experience. For the women on the row, it also means that the state will kill your friends. Now it was Melissa's turn. "I always felt there was something off about her case," Darlie said. "This woman had fourteen children! And it didn't make sense that she would harm one of them and not any of the other thirteen." Darlie contacted her attorney at the Innocence Project, Vanessa Potkin, in tears, asking her to take Melissa's case. "I told her I knew this woman was innocent. It was my gut feeling. They were going to kill her. And I couldn't take it after Lisa. I couldn't go through it again."

Potkin agreed that Melissa was probably innocent, but without new evidence, all her appeals were exhausted.

"It's a Murder"

By the time Melissa got her execution date, for April 27, 2022, Sabrina's film had been out for two years. Despite her efforts, and that of Melissa's friends and relatives, along with death penalty opponents, nothing changed except that hope had drained away.

On March 22, something did change. A Texas state representative from Dallas, Toni Rose, watched *The State of Texas vs. Melissa*, which was airing on Hulu. Rose had worked in the criminal justice system and was alarmed by what she saw. She texted a Democratic colleague in the House, Joe Moody, in El Paso, who was the cofounder of the bipartisan Criminal Justice Reform Caucus, with his Republican counterpart, Jeff Leach, who represents a very conservative district north of Dallas. Her message to each of them was: *Watch this.*

"I remember watching it on the patio," Moody recalls. "It was gut wrenching. And you're like, 'Oh my God, this lady's on the verge of being executed!'" His wife, Adrianne, turned to him and said, "You have got to do something."

Moody was struck by the fact that he hadn't heard of Melissa Lucio until now, when all legal remedies were closed to her. Legislators, especially ones concerned with criminal justice, are usually besieged by requests from lawyers when clients are approaching execution. In Texas, however, the death penalty no longer elicits a public outcry as strong as the one that attended Karla Faye Tucker.

Moody is a compact man with a large, oval head and a glistening black beard that is just beginning to gray. Respected on both sides of the aisle, he was named a "legislative hero" in 2023 for his efforts to expand access to justice. He led valiant efforts to reform gun laws following the mass shootings in El Paso in 2019 and Uvalde three years later. As soon as he finished watching the documentary, he contacted his cochair, Leach, and they wrote a letter to the Board of Pardons and Paroles requesting that they cancel the execution—thirty-one days away—by commuting Melissa's sentence or at least granting a stay. The letter cited changes in scientific evidence and Melissa's religious faith. The main point was that Melissa was not only innocent of the crime, but the crime itself did not occur.

There aren't many miracles in Texas politics, but one took place when a solid majority of the 150 members of a bitterly divided Texas House of Representatives signed the letter. It was an uprising rarely seen. By itself, the letter had no real weight. The legislature wasn't in session and was unable to act. Governor Abbott had only granted clemency once in his three terms in office, and that was after the Board of Pardons and Paroles unanimously requested it. Moody and Leach would have to reverse the tide that seemed irrevocably headed toward the execution.

On April 6, three weeks before that fateful date, members of the Criminal Justice Reform Caucus traveled to Gatesville to visit Melissa. They drove from disparate parts of the state and met in the parking lot. Warden Andrea Lozada greeted them and took them on a tour of the facility. Then they gathered in the workroom, a small windowless enclosure made of concrete bricks, entirely white like nearly everything in the facility, where the women do their crafts. The warden prayed with them, then stood in the hallway while the legislators spoke to Melissa in private. "It was a heavy space to sit in," Moody recalls. "She knew what she was facing. She could die or be free."

Toni Rose, who had aroused the representatives after watching *The State of Texas vs. Melissa,* recalled that the members had come hoping to console Melissa, but she surprised them with her acceptance of her fate. "She thanked us," Rose recalled. "She said, 'Nobody has ever fought for me before.'"

In the House members' letter to the Board of Pardons and Paroles seeking to cancel Melissa's execution, the authors singled out the "dramatic discrepancy" between the treatment of Melissa and that of her husband, Robert Alvarez, who was also responsible for little Mariah's care. He had a documented history of violence against Melissa—beating her, choking her, raping her, and threatening to kill her. In Mariah's death, he was prosecuted for a lesser crime, "causing injury to a child by omission," such as neglecting to watch over her attempt to descend a decrepit staircase.

Joe Moody and Jeff Leach convened a hearing of their committee in the Texas State Capitol on April 12. The legislature was in recess and the room was uncooled, so members of the overflowing audience fanned themselves and mopped their brows. Several of them wore black T-shirts inscribed with the message WATCH THE MOVIE. Moody was clearly agitated. Earlier, before the hearing, he visited with Melissa's son John. "He was shaking, crying," Moody later told me. He quoted John: "I haven't hugged my mom in sixteen years, and the next time they're gonna let me touch her, she'll be dead." The experience made Moody reflect on the dehumanization of people on death row—"the isolation, the lack of connectivity to people that might still love them. Is all that necessary?"

Jeff Leach said that the purpose of the hearing was to determine "whether the system can be trusted." He added, "Right now I have severe concerns about whether that's true." The real agenda for this hearing was to pressure Luis Saenz, the current district attorney in Cameron County, where Melissa was tried, into withdrawing the execution date that he requested. Before Saenz testified, however, one of the twelve jurors in that trial, Johnny Galvan, declared that he and four other jurors renounced their decision to condemn Melissa. If they had been given the information that the prosecutor had suppressed, they would have voted differently, he said. Even during the trial he thought that the defense attorney was doing very little to protect his client. Now, said Galvan, "I feel deep regret since learning about all the things we jurors were never told when we held Ms. Lucio's life in our hands." Galvan recalled that there were two votes to sentence Melissa to death. In the first one, the jury was evenly divided; "When we took the second vote I was alone in holding out for a life sentence. I felt peer pressure to change my vote. I remember one saying we would be there all day if I didn't." He concluded: "The idea that my decision to take another person's life was not based on complete and accurate information in a fair trial is horrifying."

District Attorney Saenz, who testified on video, began his remarks by noting that the case was not over. At every stage of the legal process, Melissa's conviction had been upheld, and like most death penalty cases, a flurry of last-minute appeals had landed on the state and federal dockets. Saenz noted "at least fifteen live pleadings" were still in the courts. He had no intention of acting unilaterally. Nor did he believe he had that authority.

The hearing grew quite heated. "You could go to the court and ask for the [death] warrant to be withdrawn," Jeff Leach said. "A court has never declined a request from a district attorney to do such an action."

"What legal reason would I give to withdraw the warrant?"

"I can think of many," Leach said, pointing to the five jurors who felt misled in their verdict. "Washing your hands of your ability to make this decision yourself is, to me, very, very shocking and disappointing." Leach was quoting the Roman governor Pontius Pilate, who surrendered Jesus to the mob demand that Jesus be crucified. Pilate had washed his hands in front of the crowd, declaring, "I am innocent of this man's blood."

"I am not washing my hands of this, I'm dealing with it," Saenz said testily. After the Supreme Court turned down Melissa's case on appeal, he had waited two and a half months for a motion on her behalf from her counsel before setting the death date. None came. In any case, "Even if I had the authority" to withdraw the date, Saenz said, "I will not do that." He said he disagreed with the new evidence contending that Mariah fell down the stairs and that Melissa's confession was coerced. He pointed out that those were issues that should properly be dealt with in a trial, which is exactly what the frustrated representatives believed as well, but that could only happen if Saenz withdrew the execution date.

The lawyers on the panel understood the point that Saenz was making, but his entire argument was about procedure, not about sparing an innocent woman's life. Leach argued that none of the motions or rulings the district attorney cited included the new evidence that so strongly suggested that Melissa was going to die because of legal technicalities. "I beg you," Leach finally said, sputtering in frustration. "What harm does it do to push the pause button?"—compared to the "unmistakable harm" that proceeding with an execution would do, "not only to Melissa but to our entire system of justice?"

Suppose Saenz made a special provision for Melissa, he remarked. "What do I say to the other hundred and ninety-five poor souls on death row right now?"

Moody, a former prosecutor himself, asked, "If the Court of Criminal Appeals does not issue a stay, will you withdraw your warrant?" If the CCA, the last stop on the legal journey, didn't act, the only brake on the execution might be for the district attorney to renounce his own action, an embarrassing and possible futile gesture.

"If the court does not issue a warrant and there are still motions [to be decided] I will withdraw the warrant"—a very lawyerly response, because the execution cannot go forward if there are pending motions. The hearing ended with Saenz's hedged commitment to withdraw the warrant if the courts failed to issue a stay, but there was little trust on the part of the panelists. The execution was two weeks away.

"It's not an execution," Leach told me; "it's a murder."

Patrick O'Daniel

Patrick O'Daniel

THE MAN AFTER whom the Patrick L. O'Daniel Unit is named is an effervescent tax lawyer in Austin, given to wearing green alligator boots inscribed with redheaded leprechauns, custom-made for him in a prison workshop. He was not an obvious choice to join the Texas Board of Criminal Justice, in 2017, but three years later he became chairman, a volunteer post. When he retired from that position, in 2023, the board renamed the Mountain View Unit after him, honoring his effort to change the culture of the Texas prison system. The current chair of the board, which oversees the Texas Department of Criminal Justice, Eric J. R. Nichols, told me that the goal of the Texas penal system is to have 95% of prisoners returned to their communities with a guaranteed job prior to their release.

Patrick and I were sitting with the nuns and the condemned women in the community room. Although he is no longer officially affiliated with the TDCJ, Patrick continues to visit the inmates regularly. The women seemed very lighthearted in his presence. "This is a picture of Mr. O'Daniel in the jail," Darlie told me as she passed around a spoof photo of Patrick behind bars.

Patrick loved having a joke at his expense. "Y'all didn't tell me to bring the bail money."

The TDCJ has a long way to go to be considered a decent and humane prison system. *U.S. News & World Report* ranked the state 32 out of the 50 states in corrections outcomes. It has one of the highest prison mortality rates in the country, in part because of the lack of air conditioning in more than half the units, a fault of the legislature, which refuses to fully fund the project, despite a budget surplus of $25 billion. Suicide rates in the system have doubled over the past ten years. Despite pay raises, the correctional staff is short by about a quarter.

Since 1972, when the rate of incarceration in the United States was 93 per 100,000, prison populations have boomed across the country, reaching about 2 million persons, with the highest rate of incarceration—541 per 100,000—in the world. Accounting for state and federal prisons, Texas holds about 13% of incarcerated people in the United States; when you throw in jails as well, the number reaches 18%.

Nationally, women are the fastest-growing prison population; according to the Sentencing Project, the rate of female incarceration is seven times higher than it was in 1980. More than 60% of women in state prisons have a child under the age of eighteen.

According to the Bureau of Justice Statistics, the female prison population in Texas increased 8% between 2021 and 2022, twice the growth rate of the male population.

Everyone was in a jolly mood as the prisoners were showing off their handmade Christmas decorations, which had been entered into a contest with other units. Death row came in third place. "Y'all are *so talented*!" Patrick whooped.

Earlier in the day, Patrick showed me around the unit, which comprises fifteen buildings, including seven general-population dorms, mental health and restrictive housing, and various classrooms. Patrick remarked, as we walked past a gymnasium, that it was supposed to be haunted. For years, the women in the nearest dorm claimed they could hear a basketball bouncing at night when the gym was dark and locked down. The warden, Andrea Lozada, said she heard it, too, when she was a young officer on the unit. In the old days, Patrick told me, the inmates would turn around and face the wall as prison officials walked by. It's still the case that prisoners face the wall when one of the women on death row is escorted to another building.

We stopped in at the Billman Braille Center, a large room with a hundred computer terminals, where the inmates were learning to compose in braille. The instructor told me that skilled graduates may earn hundreds of thousands of dollars a year when they finish their sentence. There was a dorm for military veterans, each of whom wore a beret and the insignia of her branch of service. They were part of a program that trains service dogs for disabled vets. We went through a school of cosmetology, and another class devoted to managing money and finding jobs. About twenty of the thirty women in the room already had a job lined up.

Patrick has a teasing, self-deprecating humor, and he was always asking the women what they needed. Because of their feedback, he had created a clinic for tattoo removal. Prison tattoos, which are usually amateurish, can be an obstacle for an ex-convict on the job hunt. "I'm not that person anymore," one woman, who had only two treatments left, explained to me. Another woman showed off her new dentures. Toothlessness had been a chronic problem in the prison; many of the women had been addicted to methamphetamines in the free world, which can cause catastrophic dental destruction. Erica had been toothless for years before Patrick created a dentistry lab in the unit. Now, one woman said to me, "you can tell which ones of us have new teeth. We're the ones always smiling."

"Thank you for having the bravery to change," Patrick said in one of the classes, after an inmate had tearfully testified about her struggles to control her damaging habits. "I'm just so proud of y'all. You are changing lives. There are so many people in the free world who wish they could say that, but they're not. They're focused on themselves. And you have something to be proud of that they'll never have."

C. F. Hazlewood

C. F. Hazlewood, deputy director of religious services for the Texas Department of Criminal Justice

MELISSA ASKED Deacon Ronnie to be her spiritual advisor when she was executed, and as the date approached, he was summoned to Huntsville to be briefed. Until recently, only an official Texas Department of Criminal Justice chaplain was permitted in the chamber with the execution team. The prison system had fought against outside religious advisors. "They said, 'We're afraid they're gonna get in there and start trying to pull the

IVs out and all that stuff,'" Ronnie told me. But Supreme Court rulings had cracked open the door to spiritual advisors who were not state employees, and those details were still being worked out in the briefing. The meeting had been scheduled to be a week earlier, but another execution, of Oliver Franklin Smith, pushed it to April 19, eight days from Melissa's death date.

They met in an old shopping mall in Huntsville that TDCJ had requisitioned for office space. Bobby Lumpkin, the deputy director of TDCJ, was there, along with Carlton "C. F." Hazlewood, deputy director of religious services. Hazlewood sized up Ronnie when he walked in and said, "Ronnie Lastovica. Are you an Aggie? Class of 1979? President of the class?" Ronnie was all those things. It broke the ice. They hadn't seen each other in forty years.

The prison authorities had developed a new set of rules to comply with the court's directive. "What they allowed me to do was put my hand on her shoulder and pray audibly," Ronnie told me. "I could bless her with holy water. A priest would have already given her last rites. And then I would just simply be present with her. I'm not there to do anything except to companion this soul unto eternal life." Before the drug began to flow, Ronnie could make the sign of the cross on Melissa's forehead.

After the protocols were explained, Chaplain Hazlewood drove Ronnie over to the Death House, inside the Huntsville Unit, commonly called the Walls, where executions take place. The prison stands in the middle of downtown Huntsville, one of seven prisons in the surrounding area, one more than in Gatesville, where the women's death row is. The Walls has loomed over the city since it opened in 1849, the first prison in the state, with towering extravivid redbrick walls, like a Looney Tunes version of a prison.

Hazlewood remembered Ronnie as "just a gentle guy, liked by everyone." Ronnie's religious side wasn't so evident in his student days. "He was just a good old Ag guy. Him and his daddy ran cattle out here in Central Texas all his life." Hazlewood assessed that Ronnie might have become a politician, having already established his electability as president of his class. "He'd walk up to any student on campus and carry on a conversation." But instead, Hazlewood said, "He just stayed Ronnie."

After the briefing, Hazlewood showed Ronnie where he could park on execution day. "There will be a line of protestors on this side," he warned, gesturing to the downtown street that runs in front of the Walls. The state maintains various houses to host families of the victim and of the killer. Ronnie was impressed by the "compassion shown to both sides." He knew that the execution process in Texas, which has put almost six hundred people to death since 1982, was "a well-oiled machine." Although death sentences have dropped to historic lows, largely because after 2005 Texas juries were offered the alternative sentence of life without parole, those who remain on death row continue their inexorable march to the death chamber.

In the final days before execution, there was paperwork to attend to—what to do with the money in Melissa's commissary account and who would pick up her property; for some prisoners, a trust fund might be established for heirs. On the morning of her death, Melissa would have breakfast in her cell in Gatesville around four a.m., then she would be taken to the visitation room for final goodbyes; after that, an armed convoy would ferry her to Huntsville. (When Karla Faye Tucker was headed to her execution, she was flown by helicopter to avoid a possible disruption on the highway.) Ronnie would meet Melissa there. They would be placed in a holding cell near the death chamber, with coffee and light snacks. A final meal would be served at four p.m. If the phone hadn't rung with news of a stay, at six p.m. Melissa would be escorted, unshackled, into the death chamber by the tie-down team, one person for each limb. She would mount the gurney, which is in the shape of a cross. Once she was fully strapped in, the IV team would establish a saline solution. There'd be no going back.

It practically never happens that the prisoner revolts on this final journey. There is little doubt that the spiritual advisor helps to keep the condemned prisoner calmer than would otherwise be the case, which benefits the prison system by making the whole process go more smoothly.

The witnesses enter the viewing portions of the chamber—two rooms, each about the size of a walk-in closet, with no chairs, separated by a glass wall inches away from the person about to die. Normally the family of the victim are opposite the inmate's feet, and the family of the inmate are at the head, but in Melissa's case it would be all the same family. Reporters may be on either side, depending on the space. When everyone is present, a curtain opens and the reality of approaching death is palpable. The lighting in the chamber is alarmingly garish and bright, like an amateur theatrical production, or a peep show.

The chamber is nine feet by twelve, painted a bilious turquoise. A prison administrator will step into the chamber and announce to the warden that he may proceed. A microphone hovers above the inmate's lips. Melissa would be asked if she has any final words. When she is done with that, Ronnie would make the sign of the cross, then the warden takes his place behind the head of the condemned and signals the executioner in the next room. The warden used to do this by raising his glasses, but that became too well known, and these days the warden pushes a button on a device like a garage-door opener that he holds in his hand. Once clicked, the executioner opens the IV flow, and the drugs take command. Minutes later, the warden would pull a sheet over Melissa's body. She would have been offered the choice of being buried in civilian clothes, but as Melissa admitted to Sabrina, she had no idea what her size was anymore. If her body went unclaimed, she would be buried in the Captain Joe Byrd Cemetery, familiarly known as Peckerwood Hill.

The bureaucratic, perversely quasi-medical nature of execution, along with the decades of waiting for the end—the lengthy premeditation—makes execution so perverse. By the time the condemned are escorted to the gurney, their crimes have been long forgotten, except by the friends and families of the victims and those of the offender, if anyone is left alive to see the sentence carried out. No matter how cruel the scene in the death chamber is, it is typically a better death than the killers gave their victims.

"The executions don't have the last say," Ronnie observed. "We fail to realize that they don't bring any sense of justice to the table. It's like, folks have buried their loved ones, but then they've also dug a grave beside them to bury themselves because of the lack of forgiveness and mercy in their lives. And now they all lay side by side."

The last time I had been in a Texas prison was in 1981, shortly before C. F. Hazlewood came aboard. A U.S. district judge, William Wayne Justice, had issued an opinion, in *Ruiz v. Estelle,* that prisons in Texas violated the Eighth and Fourteenth Amendments to the Constitution, the ones prohibiting cruel and unusual punishment and protecting due process of law. I had been in prisons in eight other states and Mexico, and the Texas system was, in the opinion of some prison advocates, one of the safest. In the previous ten years there had been only twenty-four homicides. Other systems with fewer inmates had that many killings per year. After the judge's order, Texas prisons were required to change the way they operated, and it became clear to me that the safety and orderliness I had observed were a product of the cruel and unusual actions of the authorities. Before Judge Justice's ruling, rowdy inmates were forcibly subdued, but without the threat of brutal reprisals, they began to take control. The Texas system didn't have a ready remedy. The prisons were already overcrowded, with two bunks in a cell meant for one, and often a third man sleeping on the floor. In the entire day of touring prisons jammed with inmates, I saw few guards, and only one was Black. The system was racist, and where prisons were concerned, the legislature was penurious to the point of bureaucratic sadism.

That was the situation when C. F. Hazlewood Jr. became a corrections official. Hazlewood embodies the recent history of the Texas Department of Criminal Justice. He injured his back in the Marine Corps, and in 1982 he took what he thought was a temporary prison job in Huntsville. Those were savage days. Inmates vastly outnumbered corrections officers, in some units by about 400 to 1, and they basically ran the place. In defiance of the court order, the prisons delegated the most fearsome inmates, called "tenders," to maintain order.

There was so much fighting that the halls were mopped several times a day to clean up the blood. Hazlewood worked the Eastham Unit, which was filled with gang leaders, the most dangerous inmates in the whole system. In 1986, *Newsweek* magazine called Eastham the toughest prison in America. Hazlewood had his hands full; he was stabbed twice and had his nose broken, but he didn't mind getting physical. "I was a heathen myself, and fit right in that culture," he admits.

One look and you knew Hazlewood was a tough guy—broad shoulders, deep chest, cloudless blue eyes, and an omnipresent white cowboy hat over his bald head. It would be easy to see him as a cowpoke or a roughneck, but he grew up in an academic environment. His father, C. F. Sr., was a full professor of molecular biology and physics at Baylor College of Medicine and was internationally known for his research that led to the development of MRI machines.

Eastham was designed to house about 2,600 inmates, but there were 3,500 crammed into the unit and another 900 in tents in the recreation yard. They were overseen by 13 officers per shift. "I want these guys fixed," the warden told C. F., without elaboration.

That directive would likely trigger riots, and it wasn't clear who would win in such a face-off. Moreover, Texas prisons were under federal scrutiny. Hazlewood had to find a nonviolent way of dealing with inmates for whom violence was the currency of power.

Hazlewood got a fellow officer to bring him a hognose snake from the fields. It's a common nonvenomous reptile often kept as a pet. Hazlewood walked onto the unit with the snake around his shoulders. He told the inmates it was a rattler. "They were city kids; they didn't know the difference," he recalled. He walked down the unit making sure everyone got a close look at it, then he tossed the snake into the cell of the worst offender, eliciting the reaction you might imagine. After that he would sometimes put a pinecone in a paper sack and shake it, sounding convincingly like a rattlesnake. It had an effect. The warden said, "I don't know what you did, but it was the right thing to do."

Hazlewood got promoted to manager of the TDCJ livestock operation. The Texas prison system runs the largest diversified agricultural operation in America, but even back then there were 13,000 heifers, 350,000 laying hens, 1,600 horses, as well as 1,800 tracking dogs in case of an escape. Every week the prisoners slaughtered 1,000 pigs to feed the population. "Prison was small then," Hazlewood recalls. "We only had twenty-six units. We got a hundred now."

One day he broke up an argument between two inmates in the dining room. The smaller one, known as Shorty, protested, saying, "We were just having a discussion about a Bible verse. You're a Christian, aren't you?"

"You damn right, I'm a Christian," Hazlewood said. "I live in Texas, I have a shotgun, and I drive a pickup truck. I'm a Christian."

The next night when Shorty brought him his dinner, there was a slip of paper with a Bible verse on the plate. "I called him over. I said don't do that."

"You told me last night you were a Christian," Shorty said. "I figured we'd have some fellowship."

"Bud, we're gonna have some fellowship, but it ain't the kind you're thinking about. Don't jack with my plate."

When Shorty continued to slip bits of scripture onto his tray, Hazlewood warned him, "I'm going to slap all the taste out of your mouth if you do that again, and I'll get that grin off your face." The inmate, who was Black, five-foot-two, with a ninety-nine-year sentence, replied, "Sarge, no man put that grin on my face, and ain't no man gonna take it off."

Hazlewood wasn't used to that kind of pushback from an inmate. Out of curiosity he began reading the Bible, and one day in the woods he had a conversion experience. "When I walked back to the unit the next day, I had a completely different view of the inmates. I saw them as broken people. I saw them as people who needed help."

Ronnie credits Hazlewood with affecting a change in the culture of Texas prisons. "He has humanized the inmates," Ronnie told me. "He engages them personally." Prison authorities were hostile to the changes. "They really wanted to hurt somebody; that was their way of dealing with inmates," Ronnie recalls. Hazlewood campaigned for a ministry school for the inmates, which offers a four-year program in theology. Hazlewood himself enrolled in divinity school, taking night courses. Eventually he became head of the Chaplaincy Department at the prison. In that role he's leading what he calls a paradigm shift in TDCJ. "I told some inmates yesterday, 'Fifteen years from now, when that busload of broken dreams comes in the back gate and they walk in this prison, they're gonna think it's been like that the whole time. But y'all lived through it. It's gonna come a day when people will see this as a place where they just come get treatment, and that's what I want to turn it into—get those people fixed and get them outta here, man, because it's the only way it's gonna break this cycle. I've been here long enough now that I'm seeing great-grandsons come into the prison. Yeah. I knew their great-granddad when I started working here, just a trail of crime. Sad, man, it is sad, sad, sad.' "

The Cage

THE NUNS HAD BEEN praying for divine intervention—or at least some event that would block Melissa's execution. They also prayed that they would be strong when it happened. By now they had become close to the women on "light row," as they called it, and they felt the weight of the imminent loss. "We're connected because we're sinners," Sister Pia Maria observed. "I'm not saying we killed anybody. But we're not perfect. Maybe because of our studies of metaphysics we can understand the human person better and receive them with dignity and respect, regardless of what crime they committed."

On April 23, 2022, they returned to the prison for their third visit, only four days before Melissa's execution date. This time, they came with a radical idea. The sisters had intended only to pray with Melissa before she was killed, but Sister Lydia Maria decided to also offer her the opportunity to become one of them, through an affiliation with their order called oblature. It is for laypeople who support the work of the sisters, primarily through prayer. Five hundred people around the world had this formal connection with the order. Sister Lydia asked Deacon Ronnie what he thought of the idea. He told her that if the nuns were going to invite one of the condemned ladies to become an oblate, they should offer it to them all.

When the sisters arrived in the parking lot, they immediately sensed the tension. As soon as they parked, an officer pulled in directly behind them. She had a shotgun and pointed the nuns back into their van. They had just gotten over the fright of their initial visit, and now the atmosphere was charged with the expectation of violence. They had to wait for another deacon to escort them. Because Ronnie was now a spiritual advisor for Melissa, he fell into a different category and wasn't allowed to talk to the other condemned ladies.

When the nuns entered the community room, they were shocked to see Melissa in a cage. The other women were somber and weeping, already grieving the loss of their companion four days away, and considering their own approaching execution, a burden they had been able to set aside for the past eight years.

Although the cage looked barbaric, it in fact reflected the compassion of the warden, who had stretched the execution protocols as far as possible to accommodate Melissa's last days. In the month before the execution date, Melissa was supposed to remain isolated from her fellow inmates, with a guard posted at all hours to make sure she didn't harm herself; the warden instead allowed her to stay on the row, in Cell 6, closest to the guard station. She would be allowed to remain in the presence of the other ladies but not interact with them, which explained the cage in the community room.

Sister Lydia Maria described the duties of an oblate, such as saying prayers for people who request them. These prayer intentions may arrive by phone or on the convent's website; sometimes a note might be left on the doorstep. They are posted on a convent bulletin board in what the sisters call their mailroom. The nuns incorporate these requests into their own prayers but also broadcast them to the worldwide oblate community. They told the condemned women that becoming an oblate was a path toward a "sanctified life." The new oblates would be introduced to "The

Liturgy of the Hours." Each day they could pray and sing at the same time as the nuns.

"The first one who said a big yes was Kimberly, but she said she was a Protestant and did not know if we were going to accept her," Sister Lydia Maria recalled. "I told her that our first oblate in Waco was Protestant, but that the oblature was done by saying a consecration to the Holy Trinity and also to the Virgin Mary. If she agreed with this, she could do it. She said yes, she would." Linda, Brittany, and Melissa also agreed, joining Kimberly in that first ceremony. Erica and Darlie soon joined as well.

One of the worst punishments the death penalty inflicts is the loss of meaningful work. Crafts offer the prisoners a sense of accomplishment, but little else. Becoming oblates gave the women new rules. Prayer became an occupation, a structure to fill the day, offering a mystical sense of healing themselves and the world. They prayed for people who were grieving, or injured, or seeking spiritual guidance. Although they rarely heard how things turned out, prayer gave them the feeling that they were not entirely powerless.

"We sang a few songs to lighten the mood, and as always, we said our prayer intentions to pray for each other," Sister Lydia Maria recalled. "I remember that Melissa's intention was for her son John and for each of her children. Her voice broke, but she remained strong and her peace did not leave her." She added: "The moment of farewell was unforgettable for me: I said goodbye to each one of them with a hug and I only had Melissa left to hug but we could not because she was in a cage. . . . So we stared at each other for a few seconds, and with determination and a sense of humor I said: Melissa, give me your finger, and Melissa exploded in laughter and put her finger through one of the diamond-shaped bars of the cage. I 'took' it, we laughed together, and then she said to me with much hope and strength: 'Sister, I will see you again,' and I answered: 'Amen.'"

I had to hand it to the sisters—even if the offer of oblature wasn't calculated, it was a brilliant tactical move. I had learned enough about the nuns to know that, however secluded they were, they weren't unsophisticated. They knew that executing women in Texas was a sensitive matter. They all believed that capital punishment was evil. Their commitment to assisting such despised and helpless women showed that they were willing to counter the system. I supposed that the sisters understood that it might cause an uproar for the state to kill women who could be perceived as sub-nuns—and that Texas's governor, Greg Abbott, himself a Catholic, might prefer to avoid an unwelcome controversy. Sister Mary Thomas, the vicar of the order, disabused me, or tried to, of that notion. "We did not offer them to become oblates to make execution more difficult; we did it because these are women in such a radical state. They are facing fifteen, twenty, thirty years, some of them, and they need to live in a way that can be sanctified and have meaning. But if it has political consequences, that was not our intention. We would probably lose our IRS exemption."

Sister Mary Guadalupe

Sister Mary Guadalupe

In June 2024, my wife and I attended an event at St. Jerome Catholic Church in Waco for Sister Mary Guadalupe, who was taking her final vows in the order of Sisters of Mary Morning Star. For the occasion, sisters from other states and countries attended, filling one section of the sanctuary with gray habits and white veils. Friends and family members were spread among the pews. The sisters sang some songs written by a member of the order, with beautiful harmonies. It was Sister Mary Guadalupe's official welcome into her new community, one of faith and sisterhood. Afterward, we adjourned to the community room, where a typical church lunch was spread out, with macaroni and cheese, corn pudding, and assorted carbohydrates. We found Sister Mary Guadalupe talking to her brother Arcadio (Archie) Ramos and drinking a Coors Light.

Sister Mary Guadalupe has black eyebrows above rimless glasses and her eyes are shaped like a merry jack-o'-lantern, with flat lids on the bottom and semicircles on top. She grew up in Laredo, on the Texas border, the youngest of eight children, "a very sports-oriented family," she said. She was not just a tomboy; she was the only girl in the Laredo Little League and became the city's all-star centerfielder. "I made the newspapers," she informed me. Archie added: "When the guys would come over and ask to play, they'd always say, 'and bring your sister.'" In her freshman year of high school she took up golf, then went to Texas Tech on an athletic scholarship.

Once, when I was at the convent interviewing, the prioress couldn't unscrew the top from a plastic water bottle. I confidently took it in hand and found it welded shut. A few minutes later, Sister Mary Guadalupe walked in, saw the bottle, opened it effortlessly, and drank it down. I felt pretty sheepish watching a nun best me in a contest of strength, but I learned better than to compete with her.

Like all the nuns in the Waco chapter, Sister Mary Guadalupe wears a giant watch, in her case with a white rubber strap. It's odd, because no one living in a convent needs a watch; every hour is announced by bells or chimes and never varies. I compared the nuns to the men I encountered in Saudi Arabia, who wore very similar outfits. At first glance, you think all the men are dressed identically, but a practiced eye notices the Rolex watch, the Valentino headscarf, a Montblanc in the breast pocket—little bits of class and identity that individualize the uniform. When I mentioned this, Sister Mary Guadalupe nodded in recognition. "I'm very vain about my sandals," she admitted.

A few months before, when she told the condemned ladies that she was about to take her final vows, they were surprised, because they had thought she had been a nun for a long time. "I was in another order," she admitted.

"What happened?"

"Well, they kicked me out."

This admission meant so much to the prisoners, because none of the other sisters seemed to have any failings; their lives were painted on porcelain, flawless, unscarred by sin, much less crime. It was a painful revelation for Sister Mary Guadalupe, but it drew the ladies closer to her, and that gave meaning to a low point in her life. "They were all cheering," she recalled. "They said, 'We knew it. We knew there was something about you.'"

Mary Guadalupe was born Maria Guadalupe, so she only had to make a small vowel adjustment when she became a nun (there was already a Maria Guadalupe in the order). There were eight children in her family—six girls and two boys—and Lupita, as she was called, was the youngest. She "strayed a bit" in college, by which she means she had crushes on boys. "I could have been in a lot of trouble," she told me, "but I've never gotten into a deep romance." While she was at Texas Tech, she and two friends went to Acapulco for spring break. They ran into some young men who invited them to their condo. "This boy that I was with, he could really have taken advantage of me. At one point, he tells me, 'If you want to stop, we need to stop now, because then I'm not gonna be able to stop.'" This memory made a deep impression; her virginity might have been sacrificed. "And I said, 'Yeah, let's stop.' Moments like that, I really feel God has protected me."

Melissa's Dream

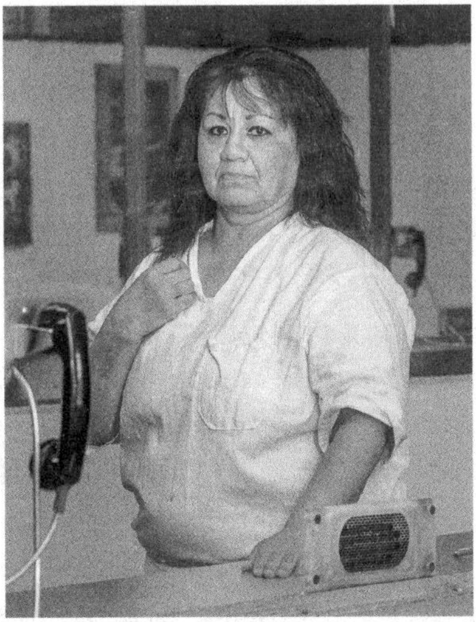

Melissa Lucio

During Melissa's final days, Deacon Ronnie's ministry was focused on her alone. The warden gave him generous access, but it was not like before. They weren't allowed to meet in the community room or right outside her cell; instead, Melissa was escorted to the visitation room in shackles, and they sat opposite each other with a pane of plexiglass between them, speaking on the phone. She told of reconciling with her mother, who had failed to protect her from family members who sexually abused her from the age of six. The visit had allowed Melissa to let go of the feelings of betrayal. During another visit with her relatives, her brother-in-law remarked, "Mel, how is it that you look the way you do? You just have this glow! This sense of peace!"

Ronnie had observed the same thing. "Anytime you get that profoundly close to death, it changes you," he said. "I could see that in her, as she was preparing to let go. It was a very sacred, intimate time to listen to her talk and replay her life through different lenses."

In his conversations with Melissa, Ronnie brought up a passage in Luke about a woman who had been hemorrhaging for twelve years. When she heard Jesus was passing nearby, she rushed into the crowd, desperate to be near him, hoping to be healed. She managed to "touch the hem of his garment" and the bleeding stopped at once. Jesus asked, "Who was it that touched me?" His disciple Peter pointed to the multitude who had gathered; it could be anyone. Jesus persisted: "Someone touched me; for I perceive that power has gone forth from me." The woman, trembling, identified herself, saying that she had touched him and had been healed. Jesus responded, "Daughter, your faith has made you well; go in peace."*

What Melissa and Deacon Ronnie made of this passage was that Melissa had found her way to peace after many years of suffering, like the nameless woman in Luke. And yet, even as she was dealing with the onrushing date of her execution, she had begun to entertain the idea that it wasn't going to happen after all. She expressed as much to her companions on the row, who humored her. Melissa had been having vivid dreams of living freely in the world. She saw herself playing with her grandchildren in the park, feeling the air stir, watching birds fly, minding children on the merry-go-round, and cooking her famous tortillas. The last time she made torti-

* Mark 5:25–34

llas was in 2007, shortly before she was incarcerated. She believed these dreams were messages from God foretelling her future, but they were also laden with regret for the companions she would leave behind. In one repeated dream she would be at her mom's house asking to use her phone to message Erica and let her know she was okay.

Melissa may have been innocent of Mariah's death, but she knew she had failed in other ways. She had been a drug addict since she was sixteen; as a young mother, she would lock herself in the bathroom for several hours a day while she took a cocaine vacation from the chaos of family life. Her drug habit imposed endless deprivation on all the people she loved, and now she was estranged from many of her children. They had endured the run-down apartments, utilities being turned off, the indignity of Child Protective Services repeatedly taking them away—to a safer place, perhaps, but to live among strangers. Melissa wished her children were babies again so she could be the parent she should have been. She prayed that they would come to the death chamber to say goodbye. It would be one more trauma in their lives, but at least they could see the woman she had become, not the mother they remembered.

In the ninety-six hours of life that remained to her, Melissa believed two things. One was that she would be executed and then reunited with Mariah in heaven. The other was that she would be spared. A few days before her execution she was escorted to the Administrative Building, where director Bobby Lumpkin was waiting, along with the warden and a chaplain. Lumpkin was there to apprise her of the execution process. "It's not going to happen," Melissa told him. "I still have to explain all of this to you, Ms. Lucio," he persisted. She said again it wasn't going to happen. He assured her that it was.

There's a scene near the end of *The State of Texas vs. Melissa* where Alfredo Padilla, one of the prosecutors in Melissa's trial, remarks, "She was given the option of doing thirty years in prison, and come out, and she chose not to. Don't blame the system, don't blame the attorneys, because ultimately it was her decision to make." His grin suggests he's amused by the irony. "She has nobody to blame but herself."

Melissa's attorney had also tried to sell her on the deal. He told her that, in thirty years, she'd be sixty-eight, still able to see her children and grandchildren. "I'm not guilty!" she cried. "I didn't do anything to my daughter." She had been so sure that someone on the jury would believe her—a single not-guilty vote and she would be free. But when the jury spoke, one after another, saying "guilty," then sentencing her to death, Melissa was in disbelief. She couldn't stop crying.

Seventeen years later and two days before her execution on Wednesday, April 27, she received a call from Jeff Leach, the state representative who had been trying to save her.

"How are you today?" he said.

"I'm good, how are you?"

"Have you heard the news?"

"No, what happened?"

"The Court of Criminal Appeals issued a stay in your execution."

Once again, a cascade of tears overtook her. "Are you serious?" she said, breaking into sobs. She could barely get words out. "What does that mean?"

"It means you're going to wake up on Thursday morning."

A Band of Mothers

Brittany

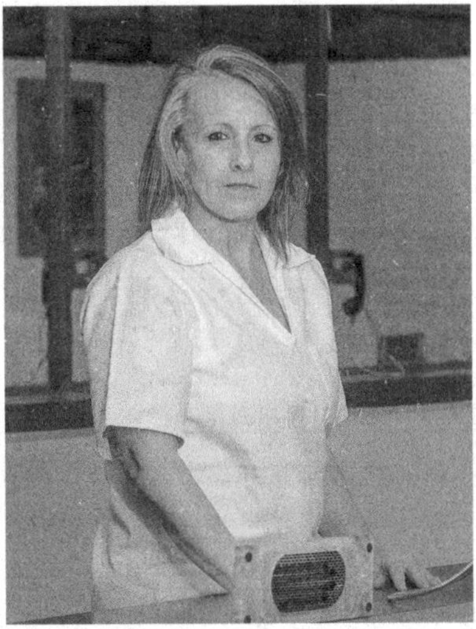

Brittany Holberg

AMARILLO IS a small town in the Texas Panhandle, near the red hills and canyonlands. Farms and ranch lands extend to the horizon. The most notable industry in the region is Pantex, where the nation's nuclear weapons are assembled. Amarillo is isolated, intimate to the point of claustrophobia, and yet it conceals a netherworld of drugs and gambling and prostitution. It was from this underground that Brittany Holberg emerged.

"Brittany was a very attractive young lady," the now-retired prosecutor James Farren told me. "Even after all the drugs, a lot of males found her attractive. And she was very good at manipulating males to get what she wanted. If that didn't work, she could always just kill them." He was proud of the conviction he secured: "Brittany Holberg was the first female ever charged with capital murder in Randall County, the first woman to ever be convicted of capital murder, and the first and only woman to ever be sentenced to the death penalty. We'll see if she actually receives it, but nobody deserved it more."

The story Farren told at the trial was that an eighty-year-old man, A. B. Towery, was walking back from Albertson's grocery store on the afternoon of November 13, 1996. He was five-foot-six inches tall, "blind as a bat," and shuffled when he walked. Farren described him as "a compulsive hand-washer" who carried Handi Wipes with him. His sons had recently taken away his car because it wasn't safe for him to drive. They didn't realize that he was saving money from his Social Security checks to buy another vehicle, which accounted for the wad of cash in his wallet.

As Towery neared his apartment, Farren told the jury, Brittany approached him and asked if she could use his telephone, offering the excuse that her boyfriend was pursuing her. Towery agreed, but once they were inside she demanded money. He refused, and they struggled. "Towery's only crime was being a Good Samaritan. And that's what got him stabbed fifty-eight times, beat with a frying pan, strangled with an electric cord, and having a brass lamp pole stuck down his throat." Actually, trial testimony also includes among the murder weapons three forks, a hammer, butcher knife, penknife, grapefruit knife, and a steam iron. Sometimes a space heater is mentioned.

Three months later, after starring on *America's Most Wanted,* Brittany was spotted outside a McDonald's restaurant in Memphis and arrested by police. Brittany then called her mother, a deputy sheriff in Amarillo, and admitted she killed Towery, but "it was not like they are making it sound." She said she had been living with Towery at the time. She told the officers she had acted in self-defense.

Amarillo police drove her back to Randall County. On the drive she said another sex worker had set up the date with Towery. She claimed she was making $2,000 a day, and her drug addiction cost her only $900 a day, so why, she asked, would she kill a man for only $1,400? Investigators claim that police had not released the information that Towery had been robbed of about that amount, but Brittany says she saw it on *America's Most Wanted*.

The trial took place in the Randall County courthouse in March 1998. Throughout the proceedings a giant photograph of Towery's massively wounded body on the autopsy table was displayed. His older son, A. B. Towery Jr., testified that, on the morning after the killing, he found his father on the floor with a lamp pole protruding from his mouth and a paring knife stuck in his abdomen. The pole came from a stand lamp that had been broken during the fierce struggle. Towery was slumped against a wall. There was blood on the floor, the walls, furniture, in the kitchen, the bedroom, the bathroom, and a closet. Brittany acknowledged that much of it was hers; she left bloody fingerprints everywhere. Towery's pockets were inside-out and his wallet, with a single dollar in it, was open on his body. Money was scattered around the apartment—$10 next to Towery's corpse, $20 in the bedroom, and $120 in the bathroom; if it was a robbery it was a sloppy one.

The sons knew that their father had been doctor shopping, getting multiple prescriptions for Sudafed, Oxycodone, and several other pain medications. Normally they would find prescription bottles in the kitchen, the bathroom, the bedside table—"hundreds of them, everywhere," according to Farren. (Nineteen empty bottles were taken to the evidence room.) The old man's eyeglasses were on the bathroom sink. Farren's theory was that the fastidious Towery was washing up in the bathroom when he heard the rattle of pill bottles being gathered. He rushed to stop Brittany from stealing his meds and that's when the fight began.

A jailhouse informant named Vickie Kirkpatrick had been placed in the same cell as Brittany. She then testified that Holberg confided that Towery was her "sugar daddy," the blood spewing from his wounds was "pretty, like a fountain," and the stabbing was "fun and amazing." Kirkpatrick explained the business of sticking a lamp pole down Towery's throat was Brittany's attempt to stop the gurgling sound he made. It sounded like Karla Faye Tucker striking again.

In an effort to refute this damning direct testimony, Brittany took the stand. She testified that Towery had been her customer for two years. On the day of the murder, when she got into his apartment, she offered to have sex. Towery agreed and gave her two hundred-dollar bills. In the fuller version Brittany told her own attorneys, Towery also gave her a glass of chocolate milk as he was unloading his groceries. As Brittany was gathering her clothes off the couch, Towery spotted her crack pipe. He walked out of the kitchen with a saucepan and hit her on the back of the head. "He made a loud breath when he hit me with it. I almost went out."

They struggled and fell into the closet. "I am screaming at him," Brittany said. "He is telling me to 'Shut up, bitch.' I freaked out. I just lost it." She pummeled him with the saucepan, and then with her fists. Towery was biting her hands. At one point he said, "If you let go of me, I'll let go of you."

Towery stumbled into a recliner chair. He was breathing heavily but still alive. "Goddammit, why are you doing this?" Brittany demanded.

The jury's eventual verdict was affected by the fact that, instead of leaving at this moment of opportunity, Brittany remained and continued the fight. She said she decided not to call the police because she was still "extremely high." It was a decision she would regret.

Towery got his breath back and they began to fight again. "He had the back of my hair," Brittany told her lawyers. Towery was hitting her in the face. "My mouth was busted open," she said. "I know that he is bleeding at this time." They wrestled from the bathroom into the dining area, until they collapsed on the floor. Brittany thought she might be having a heart attack. Crime-scene detectives would find strands of her hair that had been pulled out by the roots.

"And he was saying, 'Brittany, stop, don't hit me' . . . He was acting like I had started all this. I wouldn't quit hitting him, I wouldn't." She added: "At this point I ran in the kitchen and got a knife."

"Is it more money you want?" Towery asked. He managed to get his wallet out and threw some bills on the floor. "It was dollar bills," Brittany told her lawyer. "He had his wallet in his hand. He had a checkbook." There was a weird moment when Towery asked what Brittany wanted to do with her life. What was she going to do with her baby daughter? he asked. "What do you want to be when you grow up—a drug addict?"

"By this time, I am in the kitchen," Brittany told her lawyer. "I got the knife in my hand but I have not turned around."

"Are you still angry?" the lawyer asked.

"I was furious. I had men beat on me for so many [years]—off and on, forever—I was just mad. I didn't care."

The lawyer asked about Towery's demeanor. "He was cruel more than angry," Brittany said. "Like he had done this a million times before. He wasn't screaming loud. I guess I was the one going wild, freaking out. He kept saying, 'See, it's that shit. You are high on that shit.' I was very high. I can remember my chest hurting so bad I would sit down against the wall to get my chest to stop hurting."

"You have gone to the kitchen," the lawyer reminds her.

"And I have the knife in my hand, facing the sink," she continued. "When he said something about [her daughter] I turned around with the knife. I said, 'Don't say something about my child.'"

"What did he say?"

"'Fuck you,' then he started downing me as a mother. I went towards him and I said, 'I have a knife.' He said, 'I don't give a shit.' We were probably about as far apart as me and you are and then he stepped closer to me."

"About three feet."

"He went to push me and I started stabbing him."

"How far in did the knife go? All the way to the hilt?"

"This is so sick. I don't know."

"What happened next?"

"He grabbed my hand that had the knife in it . . . Both his hands around my hand."

"What are you doing with your other hand?"

"Hitting him. I know I hit him in the head. I hit him in the chest. I was kicking."

"Where?"

"In the shin or leg. I couldn't kick him any higher, and we fell . . . by the dining-room table, that's when we fell on the chair. The chair tumbled over and I started to reach up trying to grab shit off the table or get myself back up. By this time he basically had control of the knife. He had it in his hand. It was still in my hand by the handle."

"So he has his hand around the blade."

"Yes."

"He's holding on to the blade and it's cutting him the whole time."

"I don't know why I let go. I reached up on the table and I don't know if it was scissors or a knife that I reached for. Something else sharp in my hands. I know there were two knives involved. There was a short paring knife, black handle."

"Was that the first or the second knife?"

"Second knife."

Towery now had the first knife, which Brittany described as a serrated steak knife. Twice he stabbed her hand. "You could see the bone," she recalled. She added: "I don't remember certain things or what was grabbed and what was thrown because during this whole thing all I could feel was anger. I raged. I went into a rage. All I could see was my mother, father, my husband. And it felt like I was taking everything out on him. I just went crazy. There were at least six times that night I know of that I could have stopped and ran away, you know, ran out the door. And I wouldn't leave. It's like I thought I have to finish something. I can remember screaming, 'Mom!' He told me I was a fucking crazy bitch. He was very, very verbal, very rude."

She ran at Towery and stabbed him repeatedly. She tried to tie him up with an electrical cord. He pulled her head back by her hair and tried to stuff something in her mouth. He had the steak knife and she was fearful he would cut her throat. "We fought into the bedroom." They knocked over another table. "I grabbed the lamp that was on the nightstand."

"Where's his hands?"

"He had my hair . . . He was fixing to get that knife out of my hand and kill me . . . I remember saying 'Don't kill me.'" She pushed him onto the bed and his head hit the bed frame hard. "The man wasn't even knocked out. I remember telling him I'm sick to my stomach. And he said, "If you let go, I'll let go. And I said, 'Hell no, we have tried that before.'" She paused in her narration, then said, "I stuffed something in his mouth, y'all, and I don't know where I did it. This is where I go absolutely blank. I don't remember anything else."

She did recall striking Towery with a lamp, but she didn't specifically recall shoving the pole of the lamp five inches down his throat. That was the fatal blow; the pole nicked his carotid artery.

His body slid down the kitchen wall. Brittany stabbed him one last time because his hand moved.

And suddenly everything was quiet. "I sat there and cried for four or five minutes, and I kept saying 'Get up.' There was blood everywhere."

During the trial, Russell Towery, the younger son, had smuggled a gun into the courtroom with the intention of killing Brittany on the stand. Gil Farren, the wife of the district attorney, was the victims' assistance coordinator for the county and saw what was happening. She bravely intervened. Russell Towery later said, "If I was to have taken a shot at [Brittany], and missed, and shot the bailiff, I wouldn't have been any better than her. But I regret not shooting Brittany in the courtroom. I wanted to put Satan's daughter to sleep."

It's possible to imagine an alternate outcome of the trial, one in which the jury believed Brittany's plea of self-defense. Towery was a frequent customer of sex workers—Brittany claimed to have met him multiple times previously—and he had a violent reputation. His own son Russell once called the police when his father assaulted him with a knife. A young couple who gave Brittany a ride after the killing testified that she gave them each a hundred-dollar bill for their help, which may have been the same ones Towery had handed her. One of the bills had blood on it. Her mouth was bleeding, there was a deep cut on her thumb, and her face and neck were marked by cuts and bruises—which would likely be the case if she had been defending herself. The couple testified that Brittany had at least ten more hundred-dollar bills. Conceivably, it was cash she had earned as a prostitute or stripper. The couple offered to take her to get medical treatment, but she declined. They dropped her off near a crack house. She then spent around a thousand dollars on cocaine.

A charge of first-degree murder requires proof of intent. The prosecution held up the stolen money as evidence that she came to Towery's apartment planning to rob him. It was the aggravated offense of theft that made it a capital crime. The evidence was the open wallet on Towery's blood-soaked chest. After the trial, there was a hearing on the part of Brittany's defense to examine Towery's wallet, which Brittany claimed she never touched. If she had, there should be bloody fingerprints or DNA evidence, which could conclusively prove the theft, but there was no blood on the wallet. The appeals court ruled against the motion. Even if Brittany did not rifle through Towery's wallet and never took any money at all, she may have been guilty of robbery—solely because of presumed intent. That would be sufficient to make it a capital crime. The court also ruled that the jury could have reasonably concluded that Brittany intended to kill for the medications she stole. But there's no evidence that she actually stole any medicines; the empty bottles don't provide proof that she dumped the contents into her purse.

The damning information about stolen money came from the jailhouse snitch who later recanted, saying her testimony had been scripted by the prosecution. In her deposition, Vickie Kirkpatrick said that she had been taken from jail to District Attorney Farren's office. There was no one else in the room. Farren said, "You work with me and I'll work with you." Kirkpatrick hoped to get probation on a burglary case. She told Farren that she also had sex with Towery two or three times and that he was a "violent drunk" who treated women really badly. Farren told her she couldn't say that, because it would give Brittany grounds for self-defense. He told her to use the words "fun" and "amazing" to describe what Brittany felt as she stabbed Towery. Kirkpatrick claimed that when Farren read the affidavit that she wrote, he tore it up and rewrote it himself, then had her sign it. He also told her to testify that she did not know Towery and had never seen him before.

Religion—specifically, Christianity—is often invoked in Texas courtrooms, so that sacred and supernatural elements also figure into a jury's evaluation. During the punishment phase of the trial, a minister who worked with perpetrators said that Brittany had found Jesus in the Randall County Jail and was repentant; indeed, she was helping conduct Bible classes with the other prisoners. Farren recalled asking the minister, "Do you and Brittany ever have occasion to teach about Jesus dying on the cross for all of us?"

"Absolutely."

Farren referenced the two thieves who were crucified beside Jesus. "One of them vilified Christ," he said. "And the other thief was repentant and chastised the thief for mocking Jesus. He went on to say that he had done bad things but he believed in Jesus. And then Jesus said, 'This day you will be with me in Paradise.'" Farren asked, "If Jesus forgave him, why didn't he take him down off the cross?" Answering his rhetorical question, Farren postulated that the thief "still owed a debt to society for what he had done." Farren added: "I hope Brittany truly has had a change of heart. I hope she's a Christian. I hope I'll meet her when I get to heaven. But I still think she owes a debt to society. She's got to pay."

I asked Deacon Ronnie if justice would have been better served had Russell Towery murdered Brittany in the courtroom rather than having her wait decade after decade for the sentence to be carried out. He looked alarmed. "No, not at all! Because God would not have had time to make her into the person she became."

Kimberly

Kimberly Cargill

THE FRENZIED WOMAN who set her babysitter afire was not evident on the occasions when I spoke to Kimberly, in person or on the phone; the Kimberly I encountered was quiet and unexpectedly content, despite the fact that the psych ward was directly down the hall, and it was sometimes hard to hear Kimberly's soft voice over the periodic moans and screams. When women are admitted to the psych ward they have to walk past the sign designating death row, and sometimes they believe that's where they're going. It fills them with terror, so much so that sometimes the officers place a cover over the sign. But death row is far more peaceful than the psych ward.

The chaos, the confusion, and the hysterical outbursts emanating from that ward provide a counterpart to the tempestuous life Kimberly lived outside prison. She believes her own mental illness was the product of her relationship with her mother. "I internalized my mother," she wrote me. "I carried her with me wherever I went . . . pursued by an informal relentless chorus of furies, all with her voice—shrieking—I was worthless, shameful (unlovable) a FAILURE."

According to a psychological evaluation performed by the defense team, "Ms. Cargill's mother was violent with her approximately once per week all throughout her early, middle and late childhood." Her mother would fly into rages, Kimberly told the analyst. "I was terrified she would kill me." At age eleven, when she was crying in class, her teacher took her aside and asked what was wrong. Kimberly showed her the welts all over her back from her mother's latest assault.

Kimberly had four boys from four different relationships, all of them brief and marked by her violence. One of Kimberly's ex-husbands testified that she had set his apartment on fire. The slightest incident could set off Kimberly's rage, such as folding clothes in a manner she didn't approve of or making a sandwich that was not what she specified. When Kimberly gets mad, her sister testified, "it's like seeing the devil." Once when she was nine months pregnant Kimberly was arrested for assaulting her mother. The mother testified that she had feared her daughter would kill her. Kimberly was also arrested for harming one of her sons. (Both charges were dropped.) She would hit her children with her fists and choke them. "I thought I was going to die," her seventeen-year-old son testified. She locked her boys in their rooms for hours. One of her ex-husbands had sought custody of his child, and Kimberly's mother intervened to strip Kimberly of custody of all her children. Inevitably, Child Protective Services became involved. A hearing was to be held that could result in Kimberly losing custody of the last of the children still in her care.

Kimberly had hired a caregiver, Cherry Walker, to spend half the day watching her remaining son. Cherry was thirty-nine; she was Black, obese, and had the mental capacity of a nine-year-old. She was described in the press as "child-like." The babysitting job was part of an effort to live more independently. Kimberly learned that Cherry had been subpoenaed to testify in a custody hearing. Desperate to be seen as a calm, caring, rational mother, Kimberly made the unfortunate decision that the best way of doing that was to go off the psychiatric medicines she had been prescribed (Celexa and Klonopin for anxiety and panic disorders). She was determined to persuade Cherry not to testify. On the last day of Cherry's life, Kimberly called or left messages for Cherry seventy-three times, pleading with her to go out to dinner so they could discuss what to do.

Kimberly's version of the crime was that she took Cherry to the Posados Cafe in Tyler. Cherry was agitated about the subpoena, but otherwise the conversation was pleasant. Kimberly then headed back to Cherry's apartment after dinner, but Cherry wanted to be dropped off at a bar where she might meet her boyfriend. Kimberly refused. When she got to the intersection of South Beckham Avenue and East Houston Street, Cherry began to violently convulse, her whole body rocking, her head banging against the car window. Kimberly didn't have a cell phone to call emergency, because she had left it at home to charge. There happened to be a hospital across the street, but Kimberly didn't turn into the hospital lot because she was in the wrong lane and traffic was coming the other way. Instead, she parked at Cherry's apartment complex a block away. When she opened the passenger-side door, Cherry fell to the ground, still in the grip of a seizure.

Kimberly went from door to door in the apartment building seeking help, but no one responded. Then Kimberly, who was a vocational nurse, noticed that Cherry had stopped convulsing. She was lying facedown with no pulse. Kimberly rolled her over and performed CPR, but failed to revive Cherry. Somehow Kimberly managed to lift Cherry back into her car. She intended to go to the hospital but reconsidered when she realized that Cherry had been unresponsive for ten minutes and was clearly dead. Kimberly testified that she "knew how it would look" if she notified police. Instead, she drove around aimlessly, for about an hour, in a panic. She wound up on a deserted rural road, where she pulled Cherry out of the car, poured lighter fluid on her, and set her afire—with the intention of erasing the fingerprints she would have left after performing CPR.

The next day Kimberly washed her car to get rid of evidence, then went to the police station under the pretense of reporting a lost dog. She called friends to tell them that Cherry failed to make dinner because she had gone on a date with a White man. Then she drove out to the lonely country road where she'd left Cherry's body. "I went back to see if she was still there," she said in her evaluation. "That's when I realized it was real. Before that, I wasn't sure."

A forensic evaluation of Kimberly's mental health stated: "She described the severity of her hopelessness at the time of Ms. Walker's death, 'I was hanging on over a black hole, hanging on the cliff by my nails. Once you get to that spot, you are in trouble.' Later she continued, 'I walk the fine line between knowing I need help and shame. Between stuffing feelings and pretending to be normal and sane. All the important people in my life were conspiring against me.'"

The medical examiner was stumped. There was no soot in Cherry's lungs, so she didn't die of the fire; there was no evidence of toxins or needle marks; the scrapes were not mortal wounds, and the bruises were the kind one might expect with CPR—not what you would expect in a homicide. The medical examiner hypothesized that Cherry must have been murdered by asphyxiation, but there was no sign of choking or struggle. He ruled the cause of death as "homicidal violence through means unknown," a self-contradictory judgment. "You just ask that question, if Kimberly killed Cherry, how?" Kimberly's attorney, Kathrin Schwesinger, observed. "If that can't be answered, then you don't have proof beyond a reasonable doubt of murder. It shouldn't even be enough for an indictment."

The possibility that Cherry Walker died of an epileptic seizure was briefly addressed in Kimberly's trial but seems to have never been seriously entertained. Cherry had a long history of epileptic seizures; a neurologist testified on behalf of the prosecution that he was familiar with "sudden unexpected death in epilepsy syndrome" (SUDEP) but he had never seen it in his practice. He estimated that the chances of an epileptic dying of a seizure was less than 10%, and he didn't think it applied in the death of Cherry Walker. In any event, 10% is a lot of cases.

Given no plausible narrative of how Cherry died, the jury convicted Kimberly of murder based on the medical examiner's theory that, because she burned the corpse, she must have been guilty—somehow—of homicide. The jurors likely sentenced her to die because of the embittered testimony of her family members. Kimberly's appellate attorneys submitted a report by Orrin Devinsky, a professor at the NYU Comprehensive Epilepsy Center, who condemned the medical examiner's opinion that Cherry did not die of a seizure, even though no alternative cause of death was offered. Devinsky called Cherry's death a "textbook" case of SUDEP. "This is a sad travesty of medical care and forensic opinion," he wrote.

Linda

Linda Carty

LINDA CARTY LIVED in an isolated brick apartment building just off I-10 in far-west Houston. She had an odd profile: She was a British citizen who had immigrated to the United States from the Caribbean island of St. Kitts in 1982 to study pharmacology at the University of Houston. She taught special-needs children in a Houston elementary school while also serving as an informant for the Drug Enforcement Administration. She had a daughter when she was in her early twenties. Years later, she began a fractious relationship with a Houston man. On several occasions, she claimed she was pregnant, but no baby appeared. Eventually he told her he was "tired of lies." He moved out, and Linda panicked.

Once again she claimed she was pregnant. This time she stocked up on baby gear—a car seat, baby clothes, a crib. She pronounced a due date. She approached a neighbor, Florence Meyers, who lived in Apartment 40, on one side of Linda, who lived in Apartment 38. When Meyers was taking out the trash, she noticed Linda, who was sitting in her car. Linda waved her over. "You know I'm going to have a baby tomorrow," Linda said. "I will bring the baby tomorrow and I will show you the baby." She put her hand on her belly.

"I just knew something wasn't quite right," Meyers later told an investigator.

As it happened, Joana Rodriguez, who lived in Apartment 36, on the other side of Linda, was pregnant. Three men testified that Linda had told them that Rodriguez and her husband had a thousand pounds of marijuana in their apartment. She proposed that the men break in and steal it, but they would also kidnap Joana. Linda had come up with a story that Joana had had an affair with Linda's husband and was bearing his child. One reason she had settled on Joana as a victim is that she was Hispanic, as was Linda's husband, which would make the hoax easier to sell. According to the prosecutors, the dupes she persuaded to carry out her scheme claimed that they had no idea that, during the robbery, Linda planned to cut Joana open and take the unborn child. The men kicked in the door of the apartment. There weren't any drugs. Joana and her husband gave the robbers the cash they had in the apartment—$1,000, which they were saving to buy a new car. The men pistol-whipped Joana's husband and hog-tied him. Then they ordered Joana to follow them.

It turned out Joana had already had her baby, a boy named Ray, three days old. Linda took the child and put him in a car seat of the rental vehicle she was driving, while Joana was bound in tape and shoved into the trunk of Linda's car. In court, one of the assailants testified that he'd seen Linda placing a plastic bag over Joana's head, but that man later recanted, saying he made up the story to get a lesser sentence.

All the precautions that Linda had taken to establish an alibi turned into damning evidence. The hired robbers furiously testified against her, as did her neighbor. The baby clothes, crib, and so on made no sense for a woman who hadn't been pregnant to start with. During interrogation, the police brought in her common-law husband, Jose Corona. "Where's my baby?" he demanded.

"Are you accusing me too?" she cried. "Oh God, I'm just hoping that these people didn't kidnap nobody in my car."

Eventually, Linda led investigators to a place where she said the people who had taken her car might be hanging out. They found Joana's body in the trunk. One of the robbers was taking care of Baby Ray. He quickly accused Linda. "She conned us, you know what I'm saying?"

"Conned you into what?" a detective asked.

"She lied to us because she wanted that fucking baby."

The three men were sentenced to lengthy prison terms. Linda arrived on death row in March 2022.

Darlie

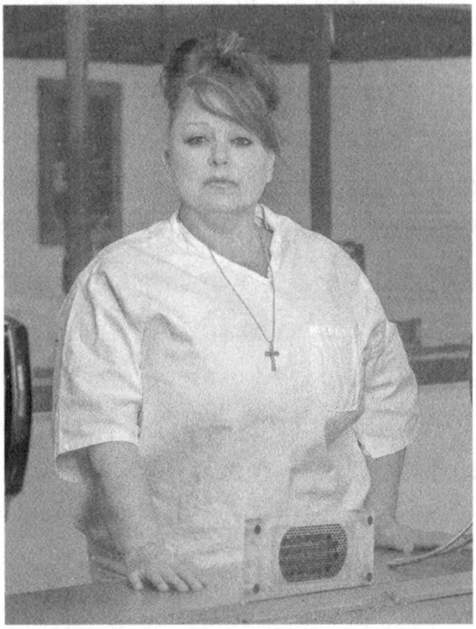

Darlie Routier

DARLIE AND DARIN ROUTIER lived in Rowlett, an upper-middle-class suburb of Dallas, in an imposing brick home with a fountain in the front yard, a Jaguar in the garage, and a cabin cruiser on the lake. Even in a city that celebrated new money they were seen as parvenus. With dyed-blond hair, diamonds on every finger, and 36DDD breast implants, Darlie might have been a candidate for *The Real Housewives of Dallas*. Yes, the Routiers were bourgeois and materialistic, but they were one couple out of countless others in Texas who finally made it and wanted everyone to know.

Darlie Routier testified she had fallen asleep in the living room of her home while watching television with two of her young sons, six-year-old Devon and five-year-old Damon. Her husband, Darin, was asleep upstairs with their baby, Drake. It was June 6, 1996.

Earlier that day, Darlie had spoken to her father in Altoona, Pennsylvania, who agreed to pick up Darlie and her family when they arrived in Washington, D.C., the following week. The plan was to tour the national monuments before heading to the mountain cabin where her grandparents would celebrate their fiftieth wedding anniversary with a massive family reunion.

Darlie said that she was suddenly awakened by Damon's cries of "Mommy! Mommy!" Someone had broken into the house. Darlie saw movement in the shadows and chased after him. She fought with the man, but whoever it was got away. Only then did she realize that the intruder had attacked her boys with a butcher knife, and that during the struggle he had turned the knife on her, causing several superficial cuts but also slicing her throat. Medical authorities said that the wound came within two millimeters of her carotid artery—the scar is still quite visible. Deeply purpled bruises covered her back, left wrist, and right arm all the way to her armpit. Her husband, Darin, heard her screams and ran downstairs, but by that time the intruder had escaped.

Two weeks later, the police arrested Darlie for the murders of her sons. They developed a circumstantial case from the scene of the crime, but the most damning piece of evidence turned out to be a video from a news crew on what would have been Devon's seventh birthday. It took place in the graveyard where the boys were buried the week before. Some of the neighborhood kids came. Darin stood beside the grave, which was covered in balloons, and Darlie, wearing cutoff jeans, the scar on her neck garishly visible, sprayed Silly String on the grave. "She was chewing gum, she wasn't crying, and it looked like she was enjoying the attention," Toby Shook, who prosecuted the case in Dallas, recalled. During deliberations, the jury watched the Silly String video repeatedly before condemning her to death. The video didn't show the moments when she wept and grieved. That material was on a secret police video that was suppressed during the trial.

Absent in the case was a plausible motive, not just for Darlie but for anyone to commit such an appalling crime. As the years passed, new information surfaced. A private investigator said that Darin failed a lie detector test, indicating that he knew the killers. The investigator alleged that Darin was deep in debt to drug dealers. Darlie told a friend she had been planning to divorce Darin. Whoever killed the boys was physically strong; the medical examiner said that the knife blows were so powerful they went nearly all the way through the boys' bodies. Most damningly, Darin confessed to Skip Hollandsworth, a fabled reporter for *Texas Monthly,* that he had sought advice from Darlie's father, Bob Kee, to find someone to break into their house and stage a robbery as an insurance scam. Confronted with affidavits from Kee and the private investigator, Darin admitted, "There's a strong possibility that was on my mind." Darin Routier has never been charged, although the same circumstantial evidence that sent his wife to death row could just as well have been used against him. (Darin has said he never carried out the plan and denies having any responsibility for the children's deaths.)

Nothing makes sense in this crime. Darlie doesn't display the pathology usually evident in the puzzling act of infanticide, nor does she have the history of trauma that characterizes most of her companions on the row. After her youngest child, Drake, was born, she suffered a kind of breakdown, her only experience with mental illness. "I started crying at a freaking Kleenex commercial," she recalled. "And that wasn't me. I was a very bubbly, very outgoing, very optimistic and fun-loving kind of person." Her depression lasted about a week, until she finally had a menstrual period for the first time since she was pregnant with Drake. She blames the depression on hormones.

Darlie's story of an intruder entering her home is supported by a bloody fingerprint no one has accounted for and a sock found in the alley with drops of the children's blood. Who would cut her own throat, especially someone as vain about her appearance as Darlie? According to her lawyer, Vanessa Potkin of the Innocence Project, the police investigator who arrived within thirty minutes of the killing quickly decided that Darlie was culpable. "You had somebody coming into court testifying that they could tell from one tiny speck of blood on the back of Darlie's shirt that somehow she was involved in a stabbing motion," Potkin said. "There were statements that somehow her own wounds were superficial. I mean, she almost died!" The consensus among the ladies on death row is that Darlie is innocent.

Taylor

Taylor Parker

On october 9, 2020, a Texas DPS trooper, Leonzel Shavers, observed a Toyota Corolla speeding west on U.S. 82, away from Texarkana toward Wichita Falls. The hazard lights were flashing. The Toyota narrowly missed hitting a pickup, then it swerved across the double-yellow line, nearly striking a bicyclist. When the trooper pulled over the Toyota, Taylor Parker waved to him frantically. The trooper approached and found a newborn baby in Taylor's lap, with the umbilical cord coiling out of her yoga pants.

The baby was turning blue around her mouth. A woman who stopped to give aid started chest compressions on the child in Taylor's lap. Then an off-duty EMT officer arrived and they attempted to cut off Taylor's pants to attend to the afterbirth, but as they were doing so, the placenta fell onto the floorboard. Meantime, the trooper found a hawk stuck under the bumper. The car must have been going really fast, the trooper figured. He pried the bird loose and it wobbled away.

In the hospital, across the state line in Idabel, Oklahoma, doctors quickly determined that Taylor had not given birth. They found bits of a glittery, purple press-on fingernail stuck to the placenta, which the prosecution argued was evidence that the real mother—twenty-one-year-old Reagan Simmons-Hancock, an acquaintance of Taylor's—was still alive and trying to claw her baby back into her body when Taylor cut her open. The baby died in the hospital. She weighed 6.68 pounds and had curly blond hair. A nurse stayed with her so she wouldn't die alone.

For years Taylor Parker had lived in a fantasy world constructed of lies, unable to confront the awful consequences of her deceit, until she was arrested and placed in the Bowie County Jail. "I was located in a cell with full light exposure, hearing inmates screaming and banging 24/7," she recalled. "I was in a full-on war in my mind. I consistently told myself you didn't do what they said. It's lies. It's someone else . . . These people are criminals, you aren't. I'd talk with myself or people who weren't there. I would come up with absurd scenarios in my mind through the day and night. I'd retreat into fictional reality and play pretend—just like I've done most of my life. It's called running from the truth."

She spent two years in jail waiting for the trial to begin, continually running the script of her innocence. Even in a jail that is used to dealing with deeply disturbed personalities, Taylor created havoc, running medical scams from the jail telephone, trying to tamper with witnesses, cutting up her jail clothing to reveal cleavage. Her defense produced a neuropsychologist from New York, Dr. Siddhartha Nadkarni, who testified that brain scans showed atrophied tissue in areas that govern behavior and executive function, which could explain her "confabulations." "It means that part of the brain is not working," he testified. "It's broken."

The medical examiner testified that Reagan had been assaulted in four or five different rooms with a claw hammer and a scalpel. She suffered five skull fractures, a broken nose, more than a hundred stab wounds. She continued to struggle as her abdomen was sliced open, the uterus cut open, and the placenta and baby taken.

Taylor didn't speak during her trial. She told a friend that when she went free she intended to get a hairless cat. "My realization came when I had to face the autopsy photos," she told me. "Jesus hit me straight on, flesh to flesh. That courtroom was so silent but I heard his voice loud and clear. He told me to open my eyes and see reality." After the sentence was pronounced, she was placed on the witness stand to hear the impact statements. "We all know you think this is about you, but it's not!" Reagan's mother, Jessica Brooks, said. "It's about Reagan and Braxlynn Sage, and the light they were while here." Jessica wore a locket with a picture of Reagan and an ultrasound image of the fetus. "My baby was alive and still fighting for her baby when you tore her open and ripped her baby from her stomach." She called Taylor "an evil piece of flesh demon."

"Every word spoken by the family I took with me that day," Taylor recalls. "Words that were meant to crush a soul, but they were true words of pain and grief and love that I needed to hear to start my road to redemption. I still carry them to this day."

The judge instructed the bailiff, "Take her to death row."

Cuffed, in leg irons, Taylor was escorted from the courthouse in New Boston, Texas, just west of Texarkana, and driven five and a half hours across north Texas to Gatesville. "My mind was a VHS tape playing forward, rewinding, and hitting play again," she said. "I sat in the back of the van and I watched my last, most beautiful, sunset turn to night and just talked to God." She was terrified of being left in the custody of the prison guards, but she supposed they felt the same way about her. Then, when she arrived at the unit, the female officer who received her told her not to be scared, she was safe.

Taylor was stripped, dressed in prison whites, then given her medical check. She was fingerprinted and each of her tattoos was photographed. When she was finally escorted onto death row she was stripped again, as is protocol when inmates move from one unit to another. She finally entered death row at midnight. "It will always be the most grateful moment of my life," she says. "I know without a doubt that Christ was right there beside me, along with the other twenty-odd guards and administrative staff, as we walked down that hallway."

There had been a moment in Taylor Parker's life when she crossed a line and became someone she didn't recognize. She had two children, but the third pregnancy was ectopic and had to be ended. This was in August 2015, "the beginning of my downfall, the path to rock bottom." She couldn't forgive the doctors for the abortion, although the fertilized egg, having implanted itself outside the uterus, would not have survived, and if it hadn't been removed it might have caused life-threatening bleeding. While she was sedated, the doctors also performed a hysterectomy.

Taylor plummeted into depression, unable to accept that she would never have children again. The fatal encounter arrived when she was at the grocery store, in 2020, in the early months of the Covid pandemic. A woman in line bumped into her. Taylor saw she was pregnant. "Thoughts were going through my head that were just not right," she recalled. "I remember being really scared of myself in that moment." An obsession—some believers might say a demon—entered her mind. She left her groceries in the cart and hurried out the store. "I went to my car and broke down." She knew she needed help but she took another path—the one that led to the cell in Gatesville.

I ran this question of demons past C. F. Hazlewood, who has given the matter quite a lot of thought. In particular, I referenced Taylor, whose crime seemed almost as if she were possessed, something I don't believe in. "Well, that's a possibility," Hazlewood said. "I went down to Haiti when I was in Bible college, and we dealt with a lot of voodoo." He also took a course in demonology in seminary. But in Taylor's case he attributed her crime to selfishness. "People way underrate that, but I know tons of people in prison because of it. They kill their wife. They want another partner. It's powerful. People use the demon thing so they have a way out—'It wasn't really me.' She got these thoughts in her mind, and that old evil heart—selfish, envy, jealousy in her heart—just came to the surface and she let that take control of her."

Taylor had been spinning stories for years; for instance, that she was the heir to a salt fortune and owned vast tracts of land. She purchased a fake "baby bump"—sold as a Halloween costume—to lend reality to her claim that she was pregnant. People who were close to her knew she was faking all along. Her mother learned of the "pregnancy" when she heard that Taylor and her boyfriend were hosting a "gender reveal" party. The boyfriend never stopped believing the story, despite an unsigned note from Taylor's ex-husband advising him that Taylor had undergone a hysterectomy and that hospitals in the region were on alert for a possible baby kidnapping.

There is a stunning TikTok video of Taylor in a hospital gown in the emergency room in Idabel. It is told entirely through the body cams of the ER docs. The police arrive, and a detective rests his arms on the sidebars of the hospital bed, patiently going through Taylor's story with her. At the beginning she is still clinging to the fiction that she just delivered a baby on the side of the road.

"Does she have a name yet?" the detective asks.

"Clancy Gaile."

"That's a nice name."

Then the doctor who examined her informs Taylor that she has not delivered a child. (They had quickly discovered that she had no uterus.) Taylor instantly constructs an alibi, saying that Reagan was the one who assaulted her. They had a terrible fight, and when her friend realized she was dying, she begged Taylor to save her baby. In a way, it was brilliant, the only possible alternative story in which Taylor is not a murderer. She told a similar story to police, including the appalling detail that Reagan's three-year-old daughter witnessed the slaughter. But in the hospital, when the cops are out of the room, and Taylor is alone except for a nurse, she wonders aloud, "There's something wrong with me. I don't know why I did it."

Now, on death row, Taylor hopes to be an advocate for women who are susceptible to the same frightful obsession. Cases of fetal abduction are rare, but they correspond exactly to the pattern established by Linda and Taylor—a prolonged pregnancy charade, intended to prevent a reluctant romantic partner from leaving, culminating in a bloody homicide of an unsuspecting mother-to-be. For five years after her hysterectomy Taylor had embedded herself in the families of friends, but gradually "I could not tell the difference between what was mine and not," she told me. "I'm not a monster. I was a broken woman who lost many parts of herself and ultimately it ended in a way I would never have wanted if I was in my right mind."

The night after she arrived on death row, she saw a kind of apparition. Six nuns stood in front of her cell. It was the last thing Taylor ever expected to see. The sisters introduced themselves. "There was a heavy atmosphere of pain," Sister Lydia Maria recalls. "We respected her silence and we hardly spoke. I was struck by the fact that she's young and very beautiful. We told her that we came from Waco to pray with her and tell her that she is not alone, that she should not lose hope in the Lord." One of the nuns had a guitar, and they sang a few songs. "She began to cry," Sister Lydia said, "but discreetly, with much pain, and without knowing her heart I dare to say with regret." The sisters promised they would be praying especially for her. As soon as they left the row, and in the middle of the hallway, in front of the guards' desk, Sister Lydia broke down. Deacon Ronnie cautioned her to get hold of herself before seeing the other women on the row. "It was a very strong and painful experience for me to have accompanied Taylor," Sister Lydia recalled, "not knowing what she had done to be in that place, to whom and how she had made someone suffer so much."

Nuns in Flight

Mary Magdalene

In 1860, in a French priory in the Bordeaux region of France, a Dominican novice named Jean-Joseph Lataste assisted in moving what was presumed to be the skull of Mary Magdalene, Jesus's closest female companion. Throughout Christian history she has been an intriguing personality, embodying the possibility of spiritual redemption. According to church lore she was a prostitute who was saved when Jesus drove seven demons from her. She is said to have spent her final years in southern France, in prayer and penance. Her skull, blackened with age, with a broken jaw, was to be transferred to a new reliquary. Lataste had the honor of kissing the skull, a moment that was to define his future ministry. "In kissing the skull formerly disgraced but today sacred," he wrote, "I said to myself: It is indeed true that the greatest sinners, men and women, have in themselves the makings of great saints; who knows if someday this is what they will become?"

Father Lataste came to preach at a four-day retreat at a women's prison in an old chateau in the French town of Cadillac in September 1864. It was sternly run by the Sisters of Charity, who condemned the inmates to total silence in the belief that they would otherwise school each other in crime. Many of the four hundred female inmates had been convicted of infanticide, some after having been raped and impregnated by their employers. Others were thieves and prostitutes with little hope of redemption. Father Lataste had the challenge of preaching to a congregation that was drained of all hope. In his first sermon, he addressed the women respectfully:

> My dear sisters.
>
> I am not sure whether you noticed: in the beginning, what I have called you: My dear sisters. My dear sisters! Do you understand that? After all, what are you to me? Yesterday I did not know you, and in a few days I will no longer see you here below. Moreover, you are fallen women . . . depreciated, banned by society if you left here. If it became known where you came from, you would be pointed out, suspect: perhaps you would be unwanted even as a servant or a charwoman. I don't approve of that; I know that it is unjust, often cruel, everything you could expect. But, that's the way things are . . .
>
> And I, a minister of God, consecrated even though unworthy to serve at His altars . . . here I am, coming to you on my own, not waiting for your call, and extending my hand. I call you: my good, my unfortunate sisters, my dear sisters.

On the third day of the retreat, Lataste spoke of his experience as a novice entrusted with the skull of Mary Magdalene. The silenced women slowly lifted their heads, "like flowers after a storm when the sun begins to touch them." Their identification with the saint was profound, giving meaning to their dream of redemption.

In his final sermon, Lataste invited the women to choose to live out their sentence by imitating nuns. "It is true that what the nuns endure by choice, you endure by force. But before God, does what was forced at first not become voluntary when it is willingly accepted?" That opened the question of what they could become when they had served out their sentence and reentered a society that despised them. Lataste envisioned a religious order that "fused" nuns of unblemished backgrounds with "rehabilitated women" from the prisons. That became the Dominican Sisters of Bethany, a name associated with Mary Magdalene. The order still operates today in France and in several other countries.

In the first half of the twentieth century, the discovery of ancient Christian and Gnostic texts in Egypt, including the thirteen papyrus codices found in Nag Hammadi, has revolutionized the understanding of the early church, especially the role of Mary Magdalene. The documents are collectively known as the Gnostic Gospels. They may have been part of a library for a Christian monastery, an ancestral predecessor of the Sisters of Mary Morning Star.

One of the Nag Hammadi texts, *The Gospel of Philip*, refers to Magdalene as Jesus's companion, whom he loved "more than all the disciples and he used to kiss her often." Another document, found before the Nag Hammadi texts, titled *The Gospel of Mary,* represents the testament of Magdalene, describing her as a favored disciple who received secret teachings from Jesus after his crucifixion. When she recounted what she had learned, Peter, the first of the twelve apostles, and his brother Andrew, scorned the idea that Jesus would confide in her rather than in his male followers. "How is it possible that the Teacher talked in this manner with a woman about secrets of which we ourselves are ignorant?" Peter demands. "Did he really choose her and prefer her to us?" Magdalene cried, "Do you think that I thought this up myself in my heart? Do you think I am lying about the Savior?" Another disciple, Levi, defended her, saying, "Peter, you have always been hot-tempered . . . If the Savior made her worthy, who are you to reject her?"

When Elaine Pagels's masterful account, *The Gnostic Gospels,* appeared in 1979, I was stirred, as many Christians and lapsed Christians were, to learn how such intriguing texts, including that of Magdalene, had been excluded from the Bible by patriarchs of the early church who diminished the importance of women in Christ's life. Among the Nag Hammadi treasures you will find this poem, "The Thunder, Perfect Mind," which appears to be an homage to Magdalene:

For I am the first and the last.
I am the honored one and the scorned one.
I am the whore and the holy one.
I am the wife and the virgin.
I am the barren one,
and her many sons. . . .
I am the silence that is incomprehensible . . .
I am the utterance of my name.

Sister Mary Thomas

From left to right, Sister Lucia, Sister Marie Nadia, and Sister Mary Thomas meeting Pope Francis

In 2001, Sister Mary Thomas, then a young novice, journeyed to the Loire Valley in France to join the Community of Saint John. She was still finding her way in religious life, despite being an extremely pious girl. "I remember at seven or eight years old being very interested in Mass," she said. "My sister would beg our mom not to have to go, she'd rather clean the whole house. And I was reminding them that there was a holy day of obligation that we weren't supposed to miss." She has no idea why she was so dutiful. "It's a mystery," she admits.

Back then she was Jennifer Leary in Murray, Kentucky, which claims the honor of being America's Friendliest Small Town. Her family had roots in County Cork, Ireland; she couldn't have been a more stereotypical Catholic girl. But in high school she fell in with a Protestant group that was on fire with faith. Jennifer was stimulated by their fervor; she even had herself rebaptized, convinced that the infant baptism of the Catholic Church wasn't valid. She came close to converting, but when it was time to choose a college, she selected Notre Dame, one of the great Catholic universities. Her father had gone there; her mother attended Saint Mary's College, the private liberal arts school for women attached to Notre Dame.

In her freshman year, Jennifer gravitated to a group of committed young Catholics. "These were jocks—strong, manly guys, leading the rosary, going to Mass every night," she said. Many of them would enter the clergy. "That environment exposed me to the idea of a vocation."

It was also her first deep exposure to nuns who were young enough that she could identify with them. She ached with desire to live meaningfully, and the nuns answered a question in her heart. "The nuns kindled in me a desire to live radically, to give my life radically to God." She came home after her freshman year and informed her parents she was going to drop out of college and become a nun. "My parents were flabbergasted," she recalls. They convinced her to finish school before she made the choice.

She dated some, but the pull toward the clergy remained strong. "Up to the very last minute of entering the sisters, I was like, I'll give God a shot. If it doesn't work out, I'll happily move on to the vocation of marriage. And for sure, I desired to meet the man of my dreams and start a family."

"I always thought I would be in an apostolic order, like teaching," Mary Thomas told me. She was outgoing, she had done well in school, and there was an apostolic order of sisters at Saint John.

But from the start she was drawn to the contemplative life. That prospect was new to her. The only contemplatives she had known before were a couple of solitary religious sisters living in a parish by themselves. It wasn't very appealing. Moreover, her father was alarmed. "God wouldn't ask that of you," he said, but she just smiled.

The Community of Saint John enjoyed an intellectual reputation within the church, in large part because of the writings of Father Marie-Dominique Philippe, the founder of the community. Mary Thomas had the opportunity to meet him several times; he was already quite elderly—eighty-nine years old when she arrived—but his friendship with literary figures, philosophers, and especially Pope John Paul II awarded him a celebrity that spilled over the boundaries of the church. On the campus of the community, he was deeply venerated.

The reality of a nun's life became apparent as soon as she entered the convent. "When I was in college, I was thinking that to live radically for Christ meant sleeping on straw mats and a kind of

Sister Lydia Maria and Sister Pia Maria

radical poverty," she said. The reality was somewhat less severe. "I was very struck by the white walls and brown wooden chairs and just one little calligraphy of a scripture verse on the wall. There's a certain sobriety that's shocking for the senses at the beginning. So when I met our order, I remember thinking, *Thank you, God, for calling me to an order that sleeps in a normal bed.*"

At Saint John, she met an older contemplative who said, "I'll pray that you persevere." Was that all? To sacrifice so much of life's pleasures—for what? Merely persevering was not her goal. "I wanted to be all in. I wanted a beautiful habit that showed the world I was consecrated." She recognized that it was expected that novices would be fervent, as she was, but would that endure for her lifetime? Would she persevere?

She also had to face the question of the utility of such a vocation. "Many people are puzzled and ask, 'Why embrace this kind of life? Is it not a waste of human energies that might be used more efficiently for a greater good, for the benefit of humanity and the church?'" She found an answer in a story that takes place in the final week of Jesus's life. There are two versions of this tale. In the Gospel of Luke, Jesus dines in the home of Simon the Pharisee, a religious movement largely opposed to Jesus's ministry. A "sinful woman" walks boldly into the dinner party, having heard that Jesus would be there. Traditionally she is cast as a prostitute. She has brought an alabaster flask of precious ointment. The scripture recounts, "She stood behind him at his feet, weeping, and began to bathe his feet with her tears and to dry them with her hair. Then she continued kissing his feet and anointing them with this ointment." Simon thought that if Jesus was a prophet, how could he fail to know what kind of woman was touching him? Jesus reprimanded him, "Do you see this woman? I entered your house; you gave me no water for my feet, but she has bathed my feet with her tears and dried them with her hair. You gave me no kiss, but from the time I came in she has not stopped kissing my feet. You did not anoint my head with oil, but she has anointed my feet with ointment. Therefore, I tell you, her sins, which were many, have been forgiven."*

In the Gospel of John, Jesus visits the home of Lazarus, whom he had previously raised from the dead. Lazarus had two sisters, Martha and Mary. Martha, the responsible one, prepared the meal, while Mary anointed Jesus's feet and then wiped them clean with her hair. Sometimes the story of the two sisters is seen as a parable detailing the difference between apostolic and contemplative nuns—Martha being the one who does the labor, preparing the meal, welcoming guests, and Mary being the one who kneels at Jesus's feet and worships him. In this version of the story, Judas is present, and he objects to the waste of such a valuable commodity. "Why was this perfume not sold for three hundred denarii and the money given to the poor?" he demands. Jesus responds, "Leave her alone. She bought it so that she might keep it for the day of my burial. You always have the poor with you, but you do not always have me."†

There is a scholarly quarrel over the identity of the woman who anoints Jesus's feet in these two similar stories, which seem to be recounting the same event. The nuns believe both are Mary Magdalene, who is mentioned twelve times by name in the New Testament, more than any other woman excepting the mother of Jesus. She was one of the women who supported his ministry, so she must have been somewhat affluent. She was present during the crucifixion and was the first to encounter the empty tomb and then the resurrected Christ. She is sometimes called the apostle to the apostles because of her closeness to Jesus.

Sister Mary Thomas interpreted the anointing as "a pure act of love, transcending all 'utilitarian' considerations." Perhaps the act

* Luke 7:36–48
† John 12:2–8

of devotion was not "useful," but it was valuable on its own terms. "Consecrated life has a link with this gesture of Mary Magdalene: we pour out the perfume of great price, we give our lives to Jesus, we consecrate ourselves completely to him, knowing that perhaps we could have done great things in the world."

In the sixth century, Pope Gregory the Great identified Magdalene as the "sinful woman" in Luke, which most modern scholars reject, but the legend of a reformed prostitute has proved to be far more appealing than that of a wealthy hanger-on. I asked Brittany if she identified with this passage about the prostitute anointing the feet of Jesus. It's clear in her response how powerfully it resonates in her imagination. "She knew where the house was all too well," Brittany wrote of the sinful woman:

> She had walked past it more times than she could count. As a woman of the city there were few doors she had not passed and even fewer she had not entered in shame. Everyone knew of her, knew what she was and what she did. It used to bother her but over time she had accepted this as her lot in life and had even attempted to pretend she did not care what others thought . . . Like every little girl, she, too, had had hopes and dreams. Those had all been shattered, though, and she had been left with nothing but the guilt and shame her sins had heaped upon her . . . She saw the way people looked at her, the way their lips turned up in disgust when they passed her on the street. Even the men she entertained treated her like dirt beneath their feet.
>
> Her profession allotted her little, but she listened to everything. Knowledge was how she survived, and this time what she had been hearing on the streets birthed a new hope. She had heard the stories of this man called Jesus. She had heard how he was healing people through the whole of Judea and all the surround-

ing country. She had heard all about him and now he was here just within the walls of a house she had dared not approach, until now. Grabbing the one prized possession she owned, an alabaster flask filled with anointment, she raced to the door and, taking a deep breath, she entered. She saw him and knew him immediately. Just the sight of him filled her eyes with tears. She could hear the whispered voices of the men reclining around him, but unlike all of the other times, this time she paid no attention. This time her entire focus was on him, and without a moment's hesitation she began to make her way towards him. Her tears began to fall onto his feet and she soon found herself falling as well and wiping her tears away with her hair . . . Then, opening the flask, she began pouring the precious ointment over his feet. She knew, with every fiber of her being she knew, that he was her hope. She felt it in a way she could not possibly explain. Nothing else mattered but this.

What began as tears of shame and despair became tears of joy as she was flooded with a love so consuming she could hardly breathe, and she knew, with absolute certainty, that everything she had done was being washed away in that moment. The world may remember, but he would not. The impossible was made possible with him and from this moment forward she would remember only the words he had spoken. "Therefore I tell you, her sins, which are many, are forgiven—for she loved much. But he who is forgiven little, loves little." The next words he spoke were for her alone and she let them saturate her soul as she stared into eyes filled with an unfathomable love. "Your sins are forgiven. Your faith has saved you, go in peace."

For some reason, when I think of the story of the sinful woman mopping Jesus's feet with her hair, it brings back to mind the image of twelve-year-old Brittany wiping up the blood of her murdered aunt.

The Community of Saint John

"I HAVE ALWAYS believed that the prayers of the contemplatives are powerful," Bishop Joe Vásquez of the Austin diocese told me. "The life of a contemplative nun is prayer. That's what they do all day long, even sometimes getting up in the middle of the night. They really do sustain the life of the church."

When he took the post, in 2010, a small group of contemplative nuns still resided in the diocese, a Dominican order known as the Poor Clares, in the East Texas town of Brenham. They supported themselves by breeding miniature horses. Each year thousands of tourists would come to watch the nuns wearing boots and cowboy hats riding around in little carts pulled by tiny horses. Afterward, the tourists would visit the gift shop, which offered crafts and ceramics. It was a profitable enterprise until age and death reduced the number of nuns to three. The miniature herd was liquidated and the cloister shuttered in 2011. "I began to think, Where can I get another group of contemplatives to be in the diocese?" Vásquez recalled. He put out the word.

In March 2017, an auxiliary bishop who was presiding over a confirmation Mass in one of the parishes spotted a nun in the congregation wearing a gray habit. She was Sister Maria Jose, who was in town to visit her ailing father. As she was slipping out of the church to find her ride, the bishop caught up to her. When she confirmed that she was in a contemplative order, he informed Bishop Vásquez. Meantime, Sister Maria Jose returned to Madison, Wisconsin, and told Sister Mary Thomas of the chance encounter. Within a couple months, Bishop Vásquez invited the nuns to visit the diocese. He was impressed. "They're kind of youthful sisters, and they just exude this joy."

The nuns sent a delegation to look over properties. There was an empty convent in Waco, abandoned by the Daughters of Charity. Vásquez thought the location would appeal to the nuns because the Sisters of Mary Morning Star already had convents in Minnesota and Wisconsin, as well as one in Saltillo, Mexico. Waco was a convenient halfway point. Moreover, the nuns were tired of snow and happy to be in a warmer climate. The first two sisters arrived in November 2020.

Before the deal was finalized, however, Sister Mary Thomas came to visit Vásquez privately. He knew that the Sisters of Mary Morning Star were a recently established order, but little else. He vaguely knew that they had broken off from another order in France; they seemed very cosmopolitan. "Most of them speak at least three languages," he recalled. Sister Mary Thomas had come to make a frank disclosure of a scandal that had pursued them and would inevitably find them again, even in Waco.

The Sisters of Mary Morning Star had a secret they dared not share with the condemned ladies. "We have also experienced injustice in front of a power that we are helpless to overcome," one of the sisters confided to me.

When I first spoke to the sisters in Waco, the prioress at the time, Sister Jeanne Thomas, was evasive about the origin of the Sisters of Mary Morning Star. I understood that there had been a break with another Catholic order in France, the Community of Saint John, which encompassed priests, apostolic nuns, and contemplative nuns. It was created in 1975 by a Dominican friar, Marie-Dominique Philippe, a charismatic theologian who died in 2006. Seven years after his death, the community quietly began to investigate an assertion that Father Philippe had abused a nun who worked as his assistant. That internal investigation cracked open a door that the Vatican had held closed for more than half a century, when Father Philippe, along with his older brother Thomas and other members of the Philippe family, who were all in the Dominican order, were secretly condemned by the church for committing numerous cases of sexual abuse over a period of seventy years. The Community of Saint John was "contaminated from its origin by a kind of 'virus,'" the report stated. Twenty-five women eventually reported acts of sexual abuse, "often as a part of spiritual accompaniments." The abuse was not limited to Marie-Dominique Philippe. The report found that, since the founding of the Community of Saint John, 167 people were victims of abuse on the part of 72 brothers. Most of the offenses were against nuns. "The slavery of women, including sexual slavery, had become part of it," Pope Francis remarked in 2019. The Vatican later clarified that the pope was not talking about actual slavery but "manipulation" that led to sexual abuse.

For several years before the shocking charges were aired, the Contemplative Sisters of the Community of Saint John, as the order was then called, had been distancing themselves from the larger religious community. They later claimed the reasons had nothing to do with abuse, which they were unaware of, but with the desire to get out from under the heavy-handed control of the priests. The church was enforcing reforms that the sisters saw as hostile. In 2009, Cardinal Philippe Barbarin, the archbishop of Lyon, replaced a popular nun who held the office of mistress of novices, which set off a rebellion. This was seen as insubordination. The nuns were told that the devil had invaded their order. An exorcist sprinkled holy water on the priory. When the new mistress took office, only a handful of sisters attended the Mass. The rest secretly packed up their belongings and fled. Other nuns in the order, who numbered about three hundred sisters in convents around the world, requested permission to leave. Within days, two-thirds of the nuns had deserted the order.

The sisters were in diaspora. Some fled to Saltillo, Mexico, where a sympathetic bishop offered refuge. Sister Mary Thomas wound up in New Ulm, Minnesota. They kept in contact, trying to regroup. In 2012, they reorganized in the diocese of Córdoba, Spain, as the Sisters of Saint John and Saint Dominic, and seventy more nuns left the Community of Saint John to join them. A few months later Pope Benedict XVI squashed the revolt, saying that "the new association has seriously undermined ecclesiastical discipline," ordering that "it is suppressed and without the possibility of being reconstituted in another form." It was a death sentence.

The sisters were no longer allowed to wear their habits. They were poor; they had no place to live, no way of making a living. Moreover, they had become scapegoats for the scandal that erupted with the release of a sensational report detailing the long-standing abuses within the Community of Saint John.

The report, "Understand and Heal: Origins and Analysis of Abuses in the Saint John Family" (*Comprendre et guérir*), was compiled internally by the Brothers of Saint John. The shock and trauma of the revelations are apparent as the writers candidly described the sordid manipulation by their spiritual fathers and other officials within the community. The report is a fascinating account of magnetism of spirituality and sexuality.

It is also a bizarre family story, beginning in 1938, when Father Thomas Philippe, a professor of theology at the Pontifical Roman University of the Angelicum, a Dominican institution, visited the convent of La Trinità dei Monti and gazed upon a charming fresco of the Virgin Mary, known as *Mater Admirabilis,* which had been painted by an aspiring nun a century before. The Virgin's eyes are downcast, apparently focused on a lily—a symbol of purity—at her feet. The colors are pinks and blues; the legend is that they miraculously softened into the pastel hues that make the image so sweet. But as Father Thomas stood before this icon of the Virgin, he was gripped by a heretical sexual fantasy.

Seven years later, in 1945, Father Thomas founded an institute, L'Eau Vive, which became a retreat for many leading Catholic intellectuals. Soon rumors arose about his teachings and sexual practices, which erupted from his mystical imagination. When church officials quietly investigated, Thomas quickly confessed that he had done "the little things," which meant "attracting people of the opposite sex to his heart," and "the big things," that is, "getting naked on these naked people." The big things occurred in a nearby Dominican convent run by Thomas's sister, Cécile Philippe. Thomas was summoned to Rome and told to cease offering communion and giving spiritual direction to women. Meanwhile, an investigation found thirty victims of the priest's sexual overtures, which consisted of "kisses, intimate caresses, fellatio, complete sexual union," most of them visited on nuns, including three mothers superior, one of whom was his sister, Cécile.

Father Thomas explained that his sexual practices derived from that fateful moment in 1938 when he viewed the fresco of the Virgin Mary. She had provided him with "mystical graces," which took hold of his body, "clearly localized in the region of the sexual organs." He perceived that Mary was not only the mother of Jesus; she was also her son's lover. In Thomas's perfervid imagination, he, too, was having sexual relations with the Holy Virgin. These fantasies he offered as "hidden mysteries" to induce the nuns to engage with him at a higher level of spirituality. When one of his victims drew back from Thomas's overtures, he told her that she had not yet arrived at the freedom of perfect love, "because in this state, every gesture, look or touch becomes indifferent, since there is no more sin, since everything is equally pure."

Father Thomas was tried by church fathers and condemned. They recommended that he be sent to a psychiatric facility or to a Dominican order outside France. His sister, Mother Cécile, was hustled out of her convent and sent to another, where she was told to keep her mouth shut. It wasn't long before the entire affair was forgotten, as intended.

~

Father Thomas was the godfather to his younger brother, Marie-Dominique Philippe. They taught together at L'Eau Vive. Marie-Dominique, usually referred to as Father Philippe, was reputed to be one of the most brilliant theologians in postwar France. He begged the church authorities to forgive his brother's "imprudence," even asserting that Thomas was a saint. But then Father Philippe was also tried and secretly condemned, forbidden to take confession or exercise spiritual direction. Within a few years he was quietly rehabilitated; and yet, like his brother and sister, Father Philippe seemed completely convinced that his sexual practices were divinely ordained. In 1975, when he was sixty-three years old, he founded the Community of Saint John.

The priest was short and slight and somewhat hunched with age. He wore thick, horn-rimmed glasses that magnified his eyebags. His forehead was high, and his hair was short and rudely cropped. Although his speech was hoarse and whispered, he radiated intelligence when he spoke, along with a kind of duality that suggested the words were coming unbidden, words that surprised even him. His manner was delicate, but his personality was confident and intriguing, which drew men to him as well, including a Polish cardinal named Karol Józef Wojtyła, who became Pope John Paul II. That friendship effectively put Father Philippe under the protection of the Vatican.

Most of the alleged abuse had taken place in the convent houses in the commune of Saint-Jodard, near Lyon, where the Community of Saint John was located. Young women came here to be trained as nuns. Sometimes they accompanied the founder when he traveled. In 1984, for instance, he led a pilgrimage to follow the footsteps of Saint Paul. "Every evening, Father Philippe heard confessions in his hotel room," one of the sisters recalled, "where all the contemplative sisters in their nightgowns went one after the other. One evening I went there too. And then suddenly, Father Philippe began to breathe in a funny way and to try to open my clothes." These assaults continued until the year before his death, in 2006, and they weren't limited to the Community of Saint John. Sisters in other orders claimed to have been abused, and laywomen as well. The vow of silence that the nuns followed contributed to the impunity for Father Philippe's actions, as did his powerful political connections to the Vatican, his reputation for holiness, and the awe with which he was regarded by women who were often fifty or sixty years younger than he. It is also true that some of the victims felt honored by his attention—they were "chosen" by a man many in the community saw as a saint.

"I think I could no longer live outside of your heart, because the Blessed Virgin gives it to me more and more," one of the nuns wrote to Father Philippe. The figure of Mary is a repeated theme in the correspondence that the investigators uncovered. At least some of the women believed that by submitting to physical love with Father Philippe they were conforming to the will of Mary. "When you touch me, it gives me Mary, who is my only life," one of the sisters wrote. "I am panting all the time."

In the 1990s, Catholicism came under assault in Europe, especially in France, with reports of rampant child sexual abuse by priests and nuns. One report claimed that 330,000 children had been abused by clergy in the French Catholic Church in the past seventy years. A beloved priest named Abbé Pierre, noted for his passionate advocacy for the homeless, had been ranked repeatedly as the most popular figure in France, but after his death his reputation was shredded by women who now felt safe to report his abuse. One after another, religious authorities were buried under the tidal wave of accusations. Against this backdrop, the report of the scandal in the Community of Saint John seemed inevitable.

The gossip caught fire in the French and Catholic press. The initial charge arose from a casual statement by an official in the community that there had been "inappropriate gestures" among the clergy of Saint John. That was in 2013, the year after the contemplative sisters broke away. A dissenting voice, that of Marie Sentis Philippe, niece of Fathers Thomas and Marie-Dominique Philippe, was drowned in the uproar. For years the nuns were pursued by rumors that were amplified in newspapers and television broadcasts. Some of the charges were verified, some were accepted on faith, and some were so fanciful or bizarre that they challenged belief. The rumors felt like a sneak attack by the brothers in the community to discredit the nuns who had fled, even as they were scattered in different countries, trying to find a way to reenter their vocation after Pope Benedict dissolved their order. The accusers said the nuns were part of a cult inside the church, that they were in denial, that they lied about their non-involvement. The nuns maintain that there was no abuse that affected them. It all seemed like an alternative reality, a dark fantasy. In any case, one of the sisters told me, "It's been an apocalypse for us."

In February 2013, a month after his edict dissolving the order, Benedict resigned and Francis became pope. He appointed a commission to see what could be done with the breakaway nuns. The following year, Francis recognized their new order, Sisters of Maria Stella Matutina (Mary Morning Star). But they continued to be shadowed by the charges leaked by the brothers in Saint John, year after year, culminating in 2023 with the publication of the shocking findings of their investigation.

"Some individuals have not been aware of the abusive nature of the acts they have suffered, or that they remain in some way under the influence of Father M.-D. Philippe," the lengthy report (more than eight hundred pages) suggests. "For example, it is surprising that to date no person belonging to the Maria Stella Matutina association has testified to abuse." The suspicious and accusatory tone of this remark would haunt the new order.

In the French press, the sisters were described as disobedient and subversive, even characterizing them as members of a sex cult. A Catholic magazine, *La Croix,* investigated the order in 2024 and concluded: "Each year, the sisters celebrate the anniversary of the death of Marie-Dominique Philippe with a special liturgy in their psalter. The 'father,' whom 25 women accuse of assaulting them, asking them to take their clothes off or performing oral sex on him, often as part of their spiritual guidance, is considered a quasi-saint in their community . . .

"How is it possible that these dissident sisters are able to lay claim to the legacy of a sexual aggressor and at the same time openly recruit novices and found new priories in dioceses throughout the world?" *La Croix* demanded. "These 300 sisters are today present on every continent. How did they manage to escape the sanctions imposed on their leaders?" The author concludes, "The Stella Matutina sisters had mastered the art of evading Roman sanctions."

Whether or not some members of the order were victimized by the founder or other brothers (for which no evidence has been produced), it's clear they are being victimized by the church—for being victims. Rumors and unsubstantiated accusations have followed the sisters, who have continually denied their abuse while losing donors and watching members walk away. One priest within the community concluded, "These women are so sexually abused they don't know they are abused."

Personal Reflections

First Church

Deacon Ronnie Lastovica

BEING WHO HE WAS, Ronnie respectfully cast his net in my direction.

"It's not such a great distance from your knees to the floor," he advised me. I told him not to get his hopes up. I admit there is a kind of intellectual arrogance, or moral cowardice, in holding myself apart from faith; at the same time, to raise my hand as a believer would mean shedding the shell of identity I had formed around myself. Religion is a powerful magnet, with a pole for attraction and one for repulsion. I have been on either end and felt its force.

Sister Mary Thomas, the vicar of the order, sent me a paper she had written as an undergraduate at Notre Dame on Blaise Pascal, the seventeenth-century French philosopher and mathematician. Pascal's goal was to show that faith is not contrary to reason, which is exactly my sticking point. He observed: "Being unable to cure death, wretchedness and ignorance, men have decided, in order to be happy, not to think about such things." As a result, Sister Mary Thomas concluded in her paper, "man will be left neither happy nor unhappy but complacent and pacified." That seems a fair description of who I am.

I grew up in the First United Methodist Church in Dallas. It was not the largest Methodist church in town, but it was sometimes referred to as the "mother church of Methodism" because of its influential pastors. My family had spent some time in a fire-and-brimstone congregation before finding our way to the more sober-minded downtown church. When I was a teenager, the pastor was Robert E. Goodrich Jr., who served there for twenty-six years before being elevated to bishop. For a preacher, he was somewhat reticent, unassuming but smooth and well-mannered, with a sincerity that radiated confident belief. There was never a moment he rang the bells of hellfire; his ministry was about compassion.

I moved away from Dallas, but as the years passed I would occasionally attend the church, usually around the holidays. The impression I had of First Church is that it would never change; it was an anchor in a tumultuous world. This was largely because of Goodrich.

In the 1950s, early in his ministry, Goodrich had a nationally televised show, which ran for nine years, titled *The Pastor Calls*. Although Goodrich is a young man in these black-and-white shows, he's already balding. When he talks, he leads with his prominent chin. His sport coat disguises the large, athletic frame of an interior lineman in his college days. His goal was to spread Christian values through dramatic enactments. He examines depression and spiritual despair. He visits a home for unwed mothers. In an episode titled "Witness," a divided neighborhood is dealing with the return from prison of a former neighbor. Some people are ready to welcome the convict home; others are fearful and want nothing to do with him. "They'll all be standing on their front porches with pitchforks," a friend of the prisoner tells Dr. Goodrich in his church office.

"What about the neighbors," Goodrich proposes to the friend. "Explain to them that, if we believe in God, we believe that God can change people. And as Christians, we ought to be able to help a man who's trying sincerely to straighten out his life." The friend is challenged by Goodrich. He summons the nerve to stand up for his friend against the bullying agitator who is stirring up the neighborhood against the returning convict. "You know, the greatest discovery any of us can make is when we discover what God can do through us when we give him a chance," Goodrich says in a voice that comes back to me after decades, friendly and inviting, quietly authoritative, full of earnestness. My father admired him intensely. He mentioned several times that he hoped Goodrich would preach his eulogy. Because of Goodrich, my father taught Sunday school, and Goodrich's daughter, Lucy, played the piano in his class. Goodrich's namesake, Robert III (Bobby), was the quarterback of my high school football team.

I had my problems with the church. Even under Goodrich, it seemed to float above the social problems of the 1960s—race, Vietnam, women's liberation—all the issues that riveted my generation. Goodrich did speak on behalf of civil rights and the right to oppose the Vietnam War, but such sermons caused dissension within the congregation. Membership declined. The belligerent politics and right-wing hate-mongering that characterized Dallas earned it the title "City of Hate." Goodrich was a voice for moderation, but not a forceful one.

As for me, I was in flight from the excessive piety of Big D and the cloud of hypocrisy that settled over the city. There were eight hundred churches in the city, including the largest Baptist, Methodist, and Presbyterian congregations in the world. In the 1960 election, W. A. Criswell, who presided over the First Baptist Church in a cream-colored suit for more than half a century, hated John F. Kennedy, warning that "the election of a Catholic as president would mean the end of religious freedom in America." Another highly amplified anti-Kennedy voice was that of H. L. Hunt, the richest man in the world and a benefactor of Criswell's church. He had three families, fifteen children, all named Hunt, and never got divorced. If the Baptists had a problem with that, I didn't hear about it.

On November 22, 1963, President Kennedy came to Dallas. It was seen as an act of political courage. That morning I picked up the newspaper on our doorstep and found a poster, with Kennedy's face and profile, over the legend WANTED FOR TREASON. The crimes he was accused of included betraying the Constitution, because he was "turning the sovereignty of the U.S. over to the Communist controlled United Nations . . . betraying our friends (Cuba, Katanga, Portugal) and befriending our enemies (Russia, Yugoslavia, Poland)." Other charges included using the National Guard to integrate schools and appointing "anti-Christians" to federal office. A full-page ad in *The Dallas Morning News* that same day echoed those very sentiments. Kennedy noticed the ad that morning in Fort Worth and told his wife, "We're headed into nut country today."

The president's motorcade passed right by Goodrich's church that morning. Goodrich and the clerical staff stood on the sidewalk and watched it pass by. My father was among the city leaders waiting at the Trade Mart for the president's lunchtime speech. As Daddy rode to the luncheon he saw *Air Force One* touch down at Love Field. Everyone in Dallas—and in America—would remember where they were when the news hit. I was in algebra class at Woodrow Wilson High School. The speech Kennedy intended to deliver was meant to challenge his reputation for weakness among the rabid right-wingers who hated him so intensely. "We in this country, in this generation, are—by destiny rather than choice—the watchmen on the walls of world freedom," he would have said at the end. "The righteousness of our cause must always underlie our strength. For as was written long ago: "Except the Lord keep the city, the watchman waketh but in vain."* Later, when I read those words, I thought he was warning Dallas—and America—of the religious hypocrisy that poisoned the politics of the era.

Two days after the assassination, on November 24, I was in church with my father and my sister Kathleen when Dr. Goodrich preached the most notable sermon of his career. It was titled "Let's Change the Climate," and it was broadcast on local television and nationally on ABC radio. As we sat in the pews, Kennedy's assassin, Lee Harvey Oswald, was about to be transferred to the county jail. A nightclub owner named Jack Ruby, with a .38 caliber Colt Cobra revolver in his pocket, mixed in with the reporters and cameramen in the basement of the Dallas Municipal Building, which housed the police department, waiting for Oswald to appear.

"Think back to September the first, 1962, the first day of fall football training in the Southwest Conference," Goodrich said at the beginning of his sermon. It was only a year before; many in the congregation knew he was referring to a mysterious epidemic, still unexplained. "It was a mild day—broken clouds, temperature in the high seventies or the low eighties—and before the day was over the SMU captain, an honor student, was dead. Several from the University of Texas were hospitalized at Austin, one of whom died within ten days. Seven were hospitalized at Texas A&M. Some were hospitalized in Fort Worth. Others were hospitalized at Rice

* Psalms 127:1

University in Houston." It was, said Goodrich, "a strange climate condition, never explained." Then the pastor began to form his indictment. "There's no question about a relationship between physical climate and life. How about the spiritual and cultural climate of a neighborhood, a city, a home?" We all understood the point he was making: Dallas wasn't innocent in Kennedy's murder. It was the climate we created that killed him—the climate of hate. After that, the "climate of hate" became the leading argument in the case against Dallas for killing Kennedy.

My father despised that sermon. Dallas was the city that had given him—a farm boy from the Dust Bowl—a chance to succeed. Here was his spiritual champion pleading guilty on behalf of the city, although it was not Dallas's right-wing fanatics who killed the president; it was a Marxist, who had previously contemplated killing Richard Nixon and had taken an errant shot at right-wing icon General Edwin Walker—exactly the kind of political crackpot who exemplified the climate of hate. I was grateful that Goodrich was taking a stand, however allusive, against the dangerous currents stirring in the city.

As Goodrich was nearing the end of his sermon, an assistant pastor walked up to the pulpit and handed the pastor a note. Goodrich glanced at it. His eyebrows shot up over his glasses. Finally he announced, "Oswald's been shot."

At home, my mother was watching the sermon on television when the network cut in to show Oswald being transferred. She watched Ruby pull his gun, step forward, and kill Oswald on live television.

For me, the drama of those days was intricately woven into the fabric of religion. In Dallas, I could see how religious piety fed political extremism. I had warmed myself on the coals of a temperate belief, only to see it rage into flames, culminating in a dramatically inevitable assassination.

Ranch Apocalypse

East of Waco, a thirty-minute drive from the convent of Sisters of Mary Morning Star, is the site of the Mount Carmel Center, where the Branch Davidian compound once stood. One day in May after a visit with the sisters, I drove out to the site. It was a beautiful morning; the trees were filled with birdsong, dickcissels and meadowlarks and indigo buntings. In this lovely place the followers of David Koresh assembled an arsenal of weapons and buried a school bus to serve as a bunker in a forthcoming holy war. Koresh predicted they were all destined to die in a giant ball of flame in the compound they called Ranch Apocalypse.

The Branch Davidians had a violent history, including gunfights and an ax murder in contests over leadership, so there was reason for law enforcement to regard the cultists as dangerous. The Branch Davidians had come to the attention of the State Department when it received a cable from a person familiar with the group that the followers were contemplating mass suicide. Then a UPS driver told the local sheriff that a package he had delivered to the compound had broken open, exposing grenade canisters. There were rumors of drug dealing and child abuse; Janet Reno, the U.S. attorney general, justified the assault because someone told her that Koresh was "slapping babies around."

In February 1993, the Bureau of Alcohol, Tobacco and Firearms attempted to serve a search warrant. That led to a shoot-out in which five ATF agents were killed and sixteen wounded; five Branch Davidians were also killed. The FBI took command of the siege, borrowing a dozen tanks, seven armored personnel carriers, three Black Hawk helicopters, and other military arms from Fort Hood. Hundreds of law-enforcement officers reinforced the siege, which lasted for fifty-one days, raising fundamental questions about religious freedom and federal overreach. Was it really the government's business if a band of armed cultists isolated themselves? What about religious freedom? What about constitutional guarantees against unreasonable searches and seizures? Having guns in Texas was certainly not unusual, although the Davidians' arsenal included weapons of war—grenades and at least two .50 caliber semiautomatic rifles. Even if rumors of child abuse were true, weren't the children in greater danger under the threat of overwhelming military force?

The standoff ended in a grotesque scene of five modified M60 tanks poking holes through the walls and pumping tear gas inside the compound—more than three hundred times—which provided the fuel that caused the conflagration that turned David Koresh's prediction into prophecy. The nation watched the immense blaze, fed by spring breezes up to thirty miles per hour, knowing that our government was killing more than seventy people still trapped inside. A woman in flames ran out of the compound, then ran back in, prompting an FBI agent to leave his armored vehicle and wrestle her to safety—an act of heroism, certainly, but what did it say about the woman's state of mind, or her commitment to her faith, that she would rush back into that inferno? Government mediators spoke to various scholars and religious leaders, but they were ill-prepared to deal with the willingness of people in an exalted mental state to die for their beliefs.

Waco instantly became a rallying cry in the rise of antigovernment militias. Attorney General Reno protested that the assault on the compound was intended to save the children, but in the event more than two dozen children died, either by suffocation, gunfire, or being burned alive. A three-year-old boy was stabbed in the chest, a possible mercy killing before being consumed by flames. Although questions remain about how the fire started, surviving members of the cult said that camp fuel had been poured in various locations in the compound by Koresh's followers to augment the catastrophe.

As the siege in Waco approached its climax, Tina Brown, the editor of *The New Yorker,* asked me to write about the conflict. I hate being in press mobs, and it seemed likely that there were more reporters than Branch Davidians in Waco. But I had been profoundly stirred by the scene of the twenty-one children who had been evacuated just before the final cataclysm. It was night; the children walked out of the compound following someone with a flashlight. They climbed into vans and passed through the perimeter of ATF, FBI, police, and military. When they rode through the flock of reporters, the children's faces were lit by the television cameras pressed against the windows. Some were toddlers; the oldest was twelve. They were entering a world they had never encountered in their young lives, a world that was intent on destroying their families and everyone they knew. I wondered what they would do with their memories.

I couldn't write about those children then; even if I could speak with them, they were still absorbing the ongoing trauma. I thought, This must have happened before.

I recalled the mass suicide of the followers of Jim Jones, on November 18, 1978, fifteen years previous. Jones, a Pentecostal preacher from Indiana, had built a following, largely in San Francisco. He was a prominent civic leader, a socialist, well known to the liberal political establishment. Civil rights leaders praised his integrated congregation. He was appointed head of the San Francisco Housing Authority in 1975. He mixed social justice with ecstatic religion, magnetizing people who were transformed by his message—and eventually, enslaved by it.

Fearing arrest and exposure as a charlatan by the press, because of his faked healings and allegations of sexual abuse by several of his followers, Jones relocated his church to a jungle in Guyana, South America. More than a thousand people followed him there, many of whom suddenly vanished without explanation—relatives, employees, officials, neighbors—gone overnight.

The community they built in the jungle was called Jonestown. Jones's followers were isolated and totally under the spell of their paranoid leader, who began to drill them in what he called "revolutionary suicide," a concept he adopted from the exiled Black Panther leader Huey Newton.

The parallels with David Koresh and the Branch Davidians were striking. In both cases, the leaders were apocalyptic evangelists who used religion to capture the minds of their followers. Each imagined the pageant of his own historic death, buffered by the sacrifice of the lives of people who loved and believed in them. In Jonestown, more than 900 people drank or were forcibly injected with the cyanide-laced Flavor Aid; nearly a third of them were children. Newspapers around the world published arial photos of the bodies, swollen in the tropical heat, splayed around the communal center with grisly artfulness.

I learned there were 85 survivors. Some had escaped into the jungle; one elderly woman had simply slept through the event. Three of the survivors were the sons of Jones: Tim and Stephan, age nineteen, and Jim Jr., who was eighteen. Stephan Jones was the biological son; Tim and Jim Jr. were adopted. They happened to be in Georgetown, the capital of Guyana, playing in a basketball tournament against the national team. The three had never told their stories before, but the horror of Ranch Apocalypse brought back memories they had kept to themselves, living quietly in the Bay Area. They agreed to talk only because Waco brought it all back.

When I first spoke with Jim Jr., he was in a deep well of denial. "I think of the good things" about Jonestown, he told me on our first meeting. "I'm sure I could tap into the memory banks of the negative torturing and abuse to people, but why?" He added: "I want to share the positive pieces of Jonestown."

"What was positive about Jonestown?" I asked.

"It allowed me as a Black man to hold my head up high," he said. "I came out of an orphanage in Indiana. Where would I be?"

He remembered returning to the United States from Jonestown. He and Tim flew into New York guarded by sky marshals, arriving in January still wearing tropical clothes. After other passengers deplaned, they were escorted to separate Winnebago trailers in a hangar and grilled for ten hours by various government agents. When the brothers got back to San Francisco, people stared at them as if they were monsters. Police followed them for months. Jim said that it was his first experience in being "leper-tized." That's what he had thought as he watched the children being evacuated from the Branch Davidian compound.

Stephan—the tallest of the sons, at six-foot-five—inherited his father's olive complexion and compelling dark eyes. His black hair was pulled into a severe ponytail; his high cheekbones emphasized the Cherokee lineage of his father's family. The question of why people would surrender their authority to someone like his father preoccupied Stephan because he sensed the same manipulative power in himself. "I've said many times, I'm glad my dad lived before me. Because I myself have experienced it. There's a willingness on the part of many people that have come and gone, who are ready to turn everything over to me—because of their own insecurity and my ability to fake confidence and strength."

Each of the sons dreamed about their father. "I had dreams of him coming after me," Jim admitted. He thought it was because he'd spoken ill of him. He guarded what he said because he had fewer bad dreams if he only remembered good things. One night at dinner in Half Moon Bay, Jim talked about how he had sent his wife, Yvette, back to Jonestown—to her death—while he remained for the basketball tournament. He couldn't have known what would happen, but the guilt lingered. Sometimes he would catch sight of Yvette in a dream, and race after her, but she would vanish. Then one night he dreamed she was waiting for him on a bench in Japantown. She said, "Goodbye, Jimmy." He said, "Goodbye, honey."

Tim Jones would agree to an interview only if his wife, Lorna, was present—he had never told her the details—but that meant we had to do it in a restaurant, where he said he wouldn't cry.

Tim was a powerful man; he could press a hundred-pound dumbbell with either hand, but he couldn't get on an elevator. The last time he tried to fly, he made the plane turn around and take him back to the gate. "I just can't stand being where I can't get out," he explained.

I asked Tim if he ever dreamed about his father. Lorna answered for him: "Every night."

His dreams scrambled the life he was living now with his life in Jonestown. Sometimes he was happy to be reunited with friends or his wife and daughter who died there. Then he would wake and remember they were all dead. Lorna said he talked in his sleep. "A lot of 'Don't! Don't do that! No!'" she said. "He thrashes around a lot."

In my long career, this was the most wrenching interview I ever conducted. Within minutes we were all in tears as Tim recounted the details of being helicoptered into the jungle, where he was made to identify the bodies of nine hundred people—everyone he knew—his natural parents, his adoptive parents (Jim and Marceline Jones), his siblings, his wife and daughter, all the people who populated his dreams. He was haunted by the belief that he could have stopped the slaughter. "I'll carry this the rest of my life—this shit wouldn't have happened!"

"What would you have done?"

"I would have killed the bastard!" he said, loudly enough that the waiter edged away and other diners studied their plates.

His memory had missing spaces in it. He couldn't remember drinking the unpoisoned potion during any of the suicide drills. For a moment he couldn't remember his dead daughter's name. He stared into space. "Monyell," he finally said.

"Is that whose baby clothes you still have?" Lorna asked quietly. He had bought them in Georgetown during the tournament. They were the only possessions he took back to the States.

"When someone asks me about someone I can't remember, and they died there, that just pisses me off beyond all means! It really pisses me off!" Tim said. It was as if the last traces of the population of Jonestown had been entrusted to his memory, and he had a duty to the dead to keep their names alive. It was all he could do to save them.

Stephan was more ambivalent about whether he could have rescued the people of Jonestown. "We were young and we were strong and we knew where the weapons were," he admitted. But there were others who could have stood in the way and they all failed.

Stephan spent years searching for dead people in his dreams. As time passed, they aged. Sometimes in his dreams he would hear that people were alive—"my mother, for example"—only to awake and grieve all over again. Other times there were moments of forgiveness. But in all the years he spent searching in his dreams he never found his mother.

His last dream of his father had been a couple years before our interview. "I was in this beautiful wooded area. It was in a time well into the future, but it was of the past." He noticed a group of people walking toward him. One man was dressed all in white—"robe, long white hair, and a walking stick. It's clear that this is good." When they finally caught up to Stephan, he recognized that the man in white was his father, grown old. "He's a man that can be trusted," Stephan thought. "He's wise and loving."

"What did you say to him?"

No words or gesture passed between them, Stephan said, "except for the love and security that I felt from the time that I saw that group, and his eyes met mine, and I woke up."

For years, when I considered these strong, appealing men, wounded but gallant in their suffering, I thought, Only religion could have broken them.

But perhaps "broken" is an unjust term. Each of the brothers continued to struggle. I thought of them as saintly in some way. They carried an unimaginable burden of grief and guilt. But Stephan's last vision of his father made me think that if Jim Jones could have been redeemed, it would not be in a dream but in his sons.

Trust

I HAD A CONVERSATION with C. F. Hazlewood about trust. By then I had met all the women, although Erica still refused to see me individually. No matter how friendly these interviews were, there was an underlying tension, a restraint imposed on the women, sometimes by their lawyers but mostly by their fear of what I might say about them. I have never felt more keenly the danger I posed as a reporter to the people I was interviewing. It wasn't surprising; their lives were hanging in the balance, and I didn't come as an advocate of their innocence. They knew I would have to write about their crimes, but I saw that as a necessary foundation of an inquiry into the possibility of redemption, if that meant anything more than a vague theological concept.

Also, I didn't know what I might find. I would be digging into their court records, talking to people who were knowledgeable about their cases, including families of their victims, forming my own judgments, which could be damning, and which could possibly turn a vote in the appeals process or spur a district attorney to seek a death warrant. The women knew this better than I.

"Erica, she's very cautious," Hazlewood told me. "She's been abused by so many men, and she flat-out doesn't trust them." His own solution was to always bring a woman with him when he was on the row, usually his wife, who is also involved in the prison ministry. In my individual interviews I was accompanied by an official escort, a discreet young woman who sat far enough apart that she couldn't hear my conversations. I don't think she affected the relationship between me and the condemned ladies.

"A big part of Erica's problem is that she is mentally slow to process stuff," Hazlewood continued. "But she's like all the women, they just don't trust people. Their thought is, This guy's with *The New Yorker*. What's he gonna say about me? They're jaded about journalists because they want the blood and guts. Say you went to Hollywood and they wanted to make a movie about Brittany killing that guy. They don't want a movie about [how] she's changed, how she lives with remorse. They want the Brittany from twenty-five years ago, a raving meth addict selling her body to the highest bidder. These women don't want that. They died to that life."

In addition to his prison work, Hazlewood has been a pastor for about four decades. Often his parishioners would question how he could spend time around such violent and hateful personalities. "You gotta realize those people who are incarcerated are no different from you," Hazlewood would respond. "Everything that's in them is in you. It's in me. I'm capable of doing anything they did. If you believe in the Bible, Jesus said that." Hazlewood referenced the scripture, Mark 7, in which Jesus reminds his disciples that the capacity to sin is human. "Out of the heart of man come evil thoughts, fornication, theft, murder, adultery, coveting, wickedness, deceit, licentiousness, envy, slander, pride, foolishness," Hazlewood said. "All these evil things come from within, and they defile a man." He continued: "You're preloaded for it. The difference is you were protected as a young child; you had guidance and you had barriers. These people didn't have that, and that element in their life came to the surface. You don't let a kid look at horror movies, you don't expose them to pornography, because you could stir something up inside that kid that you don't want, right? I mean, you look at how many child molesters were molested—

there's reality there. Part of their heart gets stirred up and then they act it out." Then he told me a grotesque story of a prisoner whose history of childhood abuse led eventually to the murder of his own three-month-old child, whom he stomped to death and then ejaculated in his mouth.

I was haunted by this story for days, and I only repeat it because I want the reader to appreciate the moral courage it requires on the part of people like C. F. Hazlewood and Ronnie Lastovica, and anyone who repeatedly faces the depravity of humankind, acknowledging the darkness but neither turning away nor surrendering to it. They expose themselves to the worst of the worst and locate within themselves the person capable of such actions. That way they can forgive the other. The nuns purposely avoid hearing about the crimes, but what a courageous leap it has been to place themselves in the company of criminals who have taken a different road. By ministering to the women, and befriending them, they ennoble each other.

The man who did the awful deed C. F. talked about demanded to be executed. "I need to be killed because you don't do what I do and live," he explained to Hazlewood, who walked him to the death chamber. "People need to know that, for something like that, you got to die." For him, execution was a form of redemption.

Communion

"THEY CALL ME the baby," Taylor Parker told me, with an engaging smile, when I was first allowed to witness Deacon Ronnie minister to the condemned women and the nuns on death row. "I'm everybody's kids' age."

Taylor was twenty-nine when she arrived on death row in November 2022, the first new occupant since Kimberly Cargill entered a decade before. When we met, she wore a puffy green jacket over her prison-issued white tunic; as far as I could tell, the jacket was the only other garment available in the prisoner's wardrobe. We talked about the two years she spent in the Bowie County Jail before being tried and transferred to death row. She had been placed in a four-cell unit for the mentally unstable. "I was with inmates who ate feces and blood," she recalled. "I wouldn't put my dog in the Bowie County Jail." She gestured to the sterile white community room with the tables and chairs bolted to the floor and the scriptural sayings on the wall. "This is the Hilton compared to the county." She adds: "I sometimes think I would choose not to leave," even if she could. "My place is to be here and tell others not to do what I did, and I've accepted that. There are consequences to our actions." She rarely gets visitors.

The religious services gave me the opportunity to meet with each of the women in person, not through a plexiglass window with a telephone receiver on each side. Linda Carty was the one who brought Deacon Ronnie into the lives of everyone in the room. "He's a gentle breeze, and he lit a fire under each of these girls," she told me. "Today they're all strong practicing Catholics." Linda herself grew up in a mixed Anglican-Catholic home but was not a steady churchgoer. "If I had a close relationship with God, I wouldn't be here today." But that didn't imply she was guilty of murder, she wanted me to know.

Linda said she had learned humility in prison. "Every time you go in and out of the unit you have to strip. You lose your dignity. At times there have been harsh, racist abuse and mistreatment, because of my ethnicity, number one"—she's Black—"and my nationality" as a British citizen.

Although Erica had refused to meet individually, she was chatty when I sat with her. "I've been here thirty-one years," she said. "I'm fifty now. I was locked up when I was nineteen." She looked scarcely older than that now, her face unlined, with a black ponytail adding to the aura of youthfulness. She is still dealing with the traumas that she believed damaged her brain, much of which she blocked out. "There's a lot of darkness there," she said. "I've been in a state of survival my whole life." Like Brittany and Melissa, she suffered repeated physical and sexual abuse. The jury heard very little of this because her attorneys failed to speak to the witnesses who could corroborate her story; moreover, the judge agreed to withhold what possible mitigating testimony there was, allowing the prosecutor to claim there was "no evidence" Erica was ever abused.

In 1997, five years after the murder that sent her to death row, Erica declared she was ready to die. She wanted to be the one to decide, not the State of Texas, so she waived her appeals. She converted to Islam and secured a burial plot in a Muslim cemetery. Bianca Jagger wrote to her, pleading with her to reconsider. Erica told her mother she would only change her mind if a miracle occurred. A few weeks before her scheduled execution, Reverend Jesse Jackson met with her. "He gave me such spiritual encouragement," Erica said. She withdrew her request to waive her appeals.

Erica was surprised to learn that the state had passed her over four times for an execution date. In the meantime, she's watched five of her companions on the row be escorted to their deaths, each leaving an empty cell behind. When one of the women gets a date, she said, "first thing we do is pray that the hearts of the judge and the courts will be changed."

Before the service, Ronnie motioned to me, and I followed him out of the community room onto the non-work-capable row, where Kimberly Cargill was the sole inmate. She stood in the dim cell behind the mesh-covered door with diagonal black bars. She had decorated her space with cards of flowers and birds. The women manage to personalize their cells with the very few items the prison permits, and each personal article is intensely valued.

"Kimberly doesn't seem to belong there," Sister Lydia Maria had written me. "She's sophisticated, well groomed, her hair is very nicely kept, clothing is very clean, she's very well read and cultivated. Her shoes are nice and different." A Bible and devotional books were stacked on Kimberly's neatly made bed; on a small metal table was an Elena Ferrante novel with a bookmark midway through; a pair of readers rode atop her gray hair. An officer once took note of Kimberly's fastidious appearance and asked, "Going somewhere?"

"The wonderful thing about reading is that it transports me," Kimberly said. She informed me she was a "fangirl" who had read several of my books. She knew much more about me than I about her, rather the reverse of the reporter's usual experience.

Kimberly held herself apart from the other inmates. She was in her forties when she was charged with her crime, unlike the others, who were teenagers or young adults, and she had intellectual interests that the others didn't share. She listens to NPR and *The New Yorker Radio Hour*. Her attorneys gave her a subscription to *Sports Illustrated*. She had a hard time making friends and asked to be moved to the non-work-capable side, where she could be alone with her books. "I could not take the stress of daily life with that group of women," she confided. "It was like being transplanted to a hostile third-world country. So for the last six months I have lived in 'Switzerland.' It is peaceful, private." Others say that Kimberly was removed because of behavioral and attitudinal problems with the other inmates. "Even to work with her, it was impossible," Melissa told me. "She was always complaining."

Kimberly later explained her situation to me by quoting one of my articles, about an elephant in the Bronx Zoo named Happy, who had been kept apart for sixteen years from other elephants. I quoted the zoo director, James Breheny, who defended the decision: "Happy has consistently demonstrated to us that she is more comfortable with her keepers and with safe barriers between her and other elephants. The stress she felt whenever in the direct company of more dominant animals had a negative impact on her welfare."

I've rarely had such an attentive reader.

When I returned to the community room, I chatted with Sister Jeanne Thomas about Kimberly. "I think it's really difficult for her to be in the group because she's overwhelmed," she said. Kimberly's mom was seriously ill, and despite their lifelong conflict, Kimberly was mourning the fact that her mother would die while she was on death row.

Ronnie was finally ready to begin. The priest was ill, so it would be a communion service, not a full Mass. Ronnie wore a white robe and cradled a cross in his arms. Brittany served as his assistant, or thurifer, to use the official term. She stood alert and eager, immersed in the timeless ceremony as the nuns repeated the Kyrie in Latin. She handed Ronnie the censer, and he waved the incense over the altar as the nuns sang. I noticed an icon that had been specially created for the women on the row; it was of Mary Magdalene behind bars. It reminded me of a conversation Sister Jeanne Thomas had with Brittany, who confessed, "Sister, I sold my body." And Sister Jeanne Thomas responded, "Brittany, prostitutes will be the first to enter heaven."

I later quizzed Sister Jeanne Thomas about this statement. She's French, and I thought there might be a language issue, but she defended it by referencing a parable, in Matthew 21, when Jesus is preaching in the temple and is accosted by the Pharisees who demand to know by what authority he is teaching. Jesus responds with the parable of a man with two sons. The father asked the first to go work in the vineyard, but he refused, although he later repented and did the work. The second son agreed to go but then did not. Jesus asked which of the sons did the will of the father? The Pharisees responded, "The first." Jesus said they had chosen correctly, but when John the Baptist had come, the Pharisees had not received him. "Truly I tell you, the tax collectors and the prostitutes are going into the kingdom of God ahead of you. For John came to you in the way of righteousness and you did not believe him, but the tax collectors and the prostitutes believed him; and even after you saw it, you did not change your minds and believe him."

I have to say I admire a parable that places tax collectors and sex workers in the same theological category.

As I watched the service I pondered: Are these women evil? If they are not, who is? One could just as easily call them insane, or temporarily so, to employ a disputed legal defense. Some of the women suffered from diminished mental capacity—Erica, certainly—and others suffered more flagrant mental disorders. I would put Kimberly and Taylor in that camp. I'm not a psychologist or a theologian, and I struggle with fitting people into categories, and yet the juries that sentenced these women to death had to make similar amateur judgments. Are they evil? Are they crazy? Is there a difference?

Another paradox was the fact that prison allowed the women a place of safety that each of them—excepting Darlie and Linda—had never really known. Here they could be redeemed versions of themselves, or as close to that as possible. Brittany and Taylor both told me that they were grateful to be on death row. "Thinking of the free world brings anxiety and fear of my past," Taylor said. "It reminds me of those things that controlled me for so long. It's the hardest thing to admit, but I do not believe in going home for myself. My place is here on the Patrick O'Daniel Unit." She added: "I stand firm on the belief you do not deserve to have something you took from another. That is part of the acknowledgment and acceptance process on the road to redemption."

I asked Brittany if she would return to being who she was if she ever got out of prison. "It's so crazy you asked that question," she said, "because a couple days ago we were all at work, and one of the ladies said, 'If none of this ever happened, where would you be in your life?' The women talked about being mothers, and one would be a doctor. When it came my turn, I said, 'I would have been dead.'" She told me that, growing up, "I felt the only place I would ever end up was in hell . . . By the time everything happened that brought me here, I was so completely broken I felt no hope. I spent my first ten years here trying to understand the purpose of my life." Now, as I watched her attending Deacon Ronnie, she appeared confident and engaged. She exemplified the transformation that Ronnie had sought in each of the women—metanoia, in the Christian sense, a personal transformation brought about by repentance. She was the person she might have been, had life been kinder to her.

At the end of service, Erica sang "How Great Thou Art." She has a deep, beautiful voice, which she trained in the choir of the Baptist church she grew up in. It was my father's favorite hymn. One of my final memories of him was at the burial service for my mother. It took place in the same Methodist chapel at Emory University, in Atlanta, where they married in 1943. At that ceremony, my father was in uniform, a young officer about to be shipped to Europe in Patton's army. Now he was an old man lying on a hospital gurney a few months before his own death. Throughout the service, I held his hand and sang that hymn in full voice, as if I believed. I had always relied on his faith as a substitute for my own.

I mentioned to Erica how meaningful her singing had been. She responded, "I'm glad I was able to minister to you today."

Bible Stories

The Gospel at Cana

From left to right, Sister Marie Elisabeth, Sister Eva Nella, Sister Mary Alix, Sister Pia Maria, Sister Lydia Maria

A PRIEST WAS RECEIVING confessions in the workroom before Mass while Sister Lydia Maria sat on the floor tuning her guitar. Lyrics for songs in Latin and English were handed out. "We can see how Larry sings," she said impishly.

When Sister Lydia had finished tuning, we sang:

Gentle Lamb, let me draw near to rest on your heart
Listen to your words and receive your secrets
There, I lay down my life
And I receive your light . . .

The next song, in Latin, was a dolorous variation of the "Hail Mary," with a complex tune that we all stumbled on. Sister Lydia Maria demanded we go through it again. "Very good," she said unconvincingly.

"Sister Lydia," Darlie said, "are y'all still making the biscotti?"

That sent Patrick O'Daniel into a reverie. "You know, the last time I had homemade biscotti, I clerked for Justice Clarence Thomas."

"Oh really!" the prisoners exclaimed.

"It's a tradition that the clerks for one justice take the other justices to lunch during the year, and for Justice Ruth Bader Ginsburg, we went to her chambers for tea, and her husband, Marty Ginsburg—he's a great chef—made homemade carrot cake and biscotti! So I have fond memories of homemade biscotti."

I had come to appreciate how eager the inmates were for personal news—anecdotes, vacations, grandchildren stories—which they received like gifts. I had been cautious about being too confiding because my life was so immensely large by comparison, and I worried that I would deepen their despair by opening a window on my happy, unbounded existence. But as my relationship with these women—and the nuns as well—developed, I decided not to be the one-way mirror that most of my reporting imposes on me. It's always a balancing act for the reporter who asks to be involved in another person's story. You know that your interest will somehow change the lives of the people you write about, but you can't calculate how much you will be changed as well. Naturally, the doom that engulfed these ladies affected me, but so did the joy in the community room among the nuns, the condemned ladies, Deacon Ronnie, and Patrick O'Daniel. Some part of each of them will always be a part of me.

Sister Lydia proposed that we do Lectio Divina, a meditative approach to a Bible reading, which has been used by monks and mystics for millennia.

“Is this going to be more Latin?” Patrick whined as the women erupted in laughter.

“No, no,” Darlie explained. “It’s really a beautiful way of going through scripture and discussing what it’s saying to you.”

The nuns asked Taylor to read a passage known as the Gospel at Cana:

> There was a wedding in Cana in Galilee, and the mother of Jesus was there. Jesus and his disciples had also been invited to the wedding. When the wine gave out, the mother of Jesus said to him, “They have no wine.” And Jesus said to her, “Woman, what concern is that to you and to me? My hour has not yet come.” His mother said to the servants, “Do whatever he tells you.” Now standing there were six stone water jars for the Jewish rites of purification, each holding twenty or thirty gallons. Jesus said to them, “Fill the jars with water.” And they filled them up to the brim. He said to them, “Now draw some out, and take it to the chief steward.” So they took it. When the steward tasted the water that had become wine, and did not know where it came from (though the servants who had drawn the water knew), the steward called the bridegroom and said to him, “Everyone serves the good wine first, and then the inferior wine after the guests have become drunk. But you have kept the good wine until now.” Jesus did this, the first of his signs, in Cana of Galilee, and revealed his glory; and his disciples began to believe in him.*

When she finished reading the passage Taylor remarked, “This always stood out to me as one of the most profound things said in the Bible, and it’s by Mary: ‘Do whatever he tells you to do.’ That’s impacted me in my life. Another thing that really stood out to me are the water jars themselves,” which were used for washing,

* John 2:1–11

not drinking. "So the effect of how something dirty can become clean—"

"And made the most delicious wine," Sister Lydia interjected.

"It's a huge thing that represents a lot, especially our redemption," Taylor concluded.

Brittany said, "The part that is so profound to me is when the headwaiter called to the bridegroom and said to him, 'Everyone serves the good wine first, and then when people have drunk freely, an inferior one. But you have put the good wine last.' That's what Jesus is to us. We have gone through life and had inferior things, but once you have had a taste of Jesus, there's nothing that compares to it."

"Nobody talks about the servers," Darlie said. "They witnessed the water being turned to wine back where nobody else was. They were told what to do—mere servers, servants, what we all are. It's so profound to me. They saw firsthand—not knowing what was going on—they witnessed the first miracle. That was the beginning, when he displayed publicly who he was. It really hits home, because we are behind the scenes, so to speak." She added: "The greatest thing about it is, in here, we get to see it all the time—he really does know our wants and our needs. I mean, there's so many things that we've witnessed firsthand that show us he really does care about the littlest to the biggest thing, because he loves each one of us."

"Mine was the first line, 'There was a wedding at Cana in Galilee, and the mother of Jesus was there,'" said Linda. "Jesus and his disciples were also invited to the wedding. How many times were they ever invited to anything? They were always persecuted. But here they were invited to attend this wedding for a reason, and the reason was turning the water into wine. I mean, the mother knew. It's amazing how a mother would know the capabilities of a child and then so confidently—like us mothers—would say, 'Hey, they're lacking wine, why don't you fill it? You know you can do it, so go do it.'"

"They could have argued," Brittany added. "He could have said, 'I'm not going to do that, I'm not that crazy.'"

"But that was his hour," Darlie said, "that was his time. That just shows you again—"

"It also shows how much he loved his mother," Brittany said. "He's telling her, 'Mom, it's not time yet,' and still he goes ahead and does what she asks."

"So this is the first miracle, but it's also the last of something," Patrick remarked. "These are the last words ever recorded in the Gospels of what Mary said. 'Do whatever he tells you.' It's like a perfect commandment on how to live your life."

Sister Lydia asked, "When Jesus answered to Mary, 'Woman, how does this concern you? My hour has not yet come,' why doesn't he just say, 'Sure, I will do it'?"

Erica had been quiet, but she suddenly observed, "Even though Mary was the mother of God, the mother of Jesus, she was still a human. Just because she gave birth to Jesus didn't mean that her humanity just faded away, and that she was just this submissive woman who kept quiet all the time. There were times when she took care of him when he was tired. There were times when she was worried about him as he was praying all night. She washed his feet when he came home from healing everybody. Those are a mother's experiences. Even though he was an adult, he was still her child."

I used to parse Bible verses in Sunday school. As I got older, it began to seem like astrology, placing more meaning on a passage than it was meant to bear. But as I listened to the women dissecting the scripture and relating it to their lives, it occurred to me that I sometimes walk too quickly past words or experiences that contain more significance than I had allowed. There is a depth to life that goes unnoticed if you move too fast. From my perspective, the lives of these women, both the prisoners and the nuns, were on pause, or frozen, but as I reflected, I imagined that the main difference between us was the absence of novelty. Most of my life floated by on an endless wave of news, travel, business, entertainment, a continual ride atop the next thing; and I loved it. But I recognized the hollowness of merely existing. By not being more contemplative, I felt ungrateful. I owed something to the gift of life.

"I had a thought," I found myself saying, uncertainly. Everyone turned to me, like stage actors startled by a member of the audience interrupting their dialogue—at least it seemed to me. "The passage starts off with a wedding, and fifty-five years ago today I was married. We're going to celebrate our anniversary tonight when I get home. But in the course of writing this story, I have gotten to know all of you in different ways, and I've been surrounded by female energy in a way that rarely happens, believe me! One of the first things I noticed is how motherhood has figured in your life and to your loss, in such a profound way."

I was just beginning to assess the price each condemned woman had paid for losing her relationship with her children. They all identified as mothers, however imperfect, but they would never embrace their children again.

I turned to the nuns. "And the sacrifice that you have made in giving up the possibility of marriage, children, family life—that has also been deeply moving, because I know how much children and now grandchildren have meant to me."

There was a prolonged silence after I spoke, which made me wonder if I had made a mistake by stepping out of my role, but it passed without comment.

Patrick had slipped out to go to confession, but in just a few minutes he returned, to general surprise. "You must be real good," one of the women said, meaning he had returned so quickly he must have little reason to confess. "Oh no, I always keep a list," he said, pulling a card out of his pocket. That set off a wave of guffaws from the women, including the nuns. Patrick explained: "You see, the more you confess, the more you realize, 'Oh my goodness, I forgot some sins!' You need to write them down on your sin list so you can get through them quick."

After Mass, Erica sang "Amazing Grace."

As we were breaking up, I went down the non-work-capable row to say hello to Kimberly in her solitary cell, and Patrick came along. It was January and the row was frigid. "A few weeks of freezing is worth the eight months of air conditioning," said Kimberly. "So when I'm freezing, that's what I think about."

I could see that Patrick was chagrined. "I will tell you this," he said, "as of a few months ago everywhere in this unit is air conditioned. So you're not the only one with air conditioning. But yes, it's cold in the winter."

"I think the cold spells are almost over," Kimberly said graciously. "Just one or two more."

Patrick admired how she had decorated her cell with postcards. "Warden Lozada let us start doing it," she said. "It makes a huge difference. Everywhere I look, I see things that I love. In my little box, I have flowers and hummingbirds and sunsets. And then there's Mother Teresa above my mirror." We talked a bit about her state of mind. We had spoken on the phone a few days before, and she was in tears again. "I got some difficult news," she explained to Patrick. Her legal challenge had failed, and she could expect an execution date at any point. "I was struggling a little bit. But what was interesting is that Sister Pia Maria came up to my cell with Deacon Ronnie, and she said, 'Do you write poetry?' I said no, I wrote something about my dog when I was about nine and two love poems when I was a teenager. And she said, 'I would really like you to write a poem about hope, based on scripture.' I spent, like, three days reading all the scriptures about hope. So doing something for someone else ended up blessing me, and this was the result."

Kimberly sent the poem to me and asked that I forward it to Sister Pia Maria. Here is a part of it:

> *Nothing is perfect in this broken, sinful world*
> *Full of lost and lonely people*
> *Except our Lord's Word*
> *Just waiting to be shared and heard.*
> *His Word breathes Life into me, showing me from above*
> *Grace, the Hidden Treasure of His Soul.*
> *My Hope is the essence of His Love.*

Darlie wrote me the next day to say that, after I left, an officer came down their row and gave each of the women two long-stemmed roses. "I started crying. It has been twenty-eight years since I've held a rose. They told us they were from Mr. O'Daniel. A simple gesture for some but nothing simple to us. I have my roses in a water bottle right on the side of my bed and I can't stop looking at them, smelling them. I don't think I will ever look at a rose the same."

Jesus in the Dock

KINKY FRIEDMAN WAS a writer and musician who fronted a band called Kinky Friedman and the Texas Jewboys. He was a wildly irreverent solitary misogynist who converted his family ranch into a never-kill sanctuary for abused and abandoned animals that would otherwise be put down. He described it as "a court of last resort for those at death's door."

He was less concerned about the death penalty for humans, until he interviewed Max Soffar, who was on death row for a triple murder, in 1980, in a Houston bowling alley. One victim, shot in the head, survived to testify against him. Kinky interviewed Soffar in prison for a *Texas Monthly* story and was immediately persuaded of his innocence. "I'm not anti-death-penalty," Kinky said at the time, "but I damn sure am anti-the-wrong-guy-getting-executed."

In 2006, he announced he was running for governor, against Rick Perry, the Republican incumbent, and a crowded Democratic field. He had several wonderful campaign slogans, including "How Hard Can It Be?" and "Why the Hell Not?" (He would wind up with 12.6% of the vote, fourth in a field of six.) Most voters thought his campaign was a Kinky-esque comedy. This was a man whose best-known song was "They Ain't Makin' Jews Like Jesus Anymore."

Kinky took a break from his gubernatorial campaign to testify for Soffar, whose original conviction had been overturned. The jury convicted him a second time. (He would die of liver cancer before his execution.) At every stop on his campaign voters would ask Kinky about his stance on execution. It was a relevant question in Texas, where the governor has the final say over granting clemency when recommended by the Board of Pardons and Paroles. Kinky was now arguing that the system of justice wasn't perfect and never would be.

I ran into him that fall during the Texas Book Festival. The candidate was still sorting out his thoughts about the death penalty; at the time, he was calling for a moratorium on executions. "When was the last rich man executed in Texas?" he asked. But he hadn't come up with a firm position pro or con until he got to the little Hill Country town of Kerrville, and one of the cowboys in the audience asked him once again where he stood on the death penalty.

"Well, I'm against it," he finally declared. "And it's because the government executed an innocent man. His name was Jesus Christ."

Mark Osler is a former prosecutor who now teaches law at the University of St. Thomas in Minneapolis. Before that, he taught at Baylor University in Waco. Despite being a new professor at the largest Baptist university in the world, Osler decided to stage a mock trial of Jesus under modern Texas law. The trial was held in a church over the course of four Sundays, with Osler serving as the prosecutor, and another law professor playing the role of Jesus's defense attorney. The congregation was the jury.

Osler took the congregation/jury down the road to crucifixion step by step, showing how, "to a remarkable degree," the story of Christ replicates the structures and weaknesses of current criminal law. The arrest was facilitated by a paid informant—Judas, one of the twelve disciples, foreseen by Jesus as the one who would betray him. Judas had sought out authorities, asking, "What will you give me if I betray him to you?"* He was awarded thirty pieces of silver, and his name became eternally damned. The arrest happened just before dawn—a time-honored practice of police agencies for dangerous suspects. "See, my betrayer is at hand," Jesus said as Judas arrived with a mob led by "priests, scribes and elders."† Jesus was bound and taken to the home of Annas, a prominent judge as well as the father-in-law of Caiaphas, the high priest. In Osler's comparison, Annas plays the role of magistrate, who advises the defendant of the charges against him. In Texas, the magistrate can be a justice of the peace or a mayor or even a justice of the state supreme court. Annas informed Jesus that he had been accused of blasphemy for claiming to be the Messiah—meaning the anointed one, the heir to the throne of King David—and of scheming to destroy the temple in Jerusalem, the center of Jewish worship. Jesus complained that he had done nothing in secret; he had spoken openly in the temple. "Why do you ask me?" he said. "Ask those who heard me."‡ A guard who thought Jesus was being insolent struck him in the face, the first of many beatings Jesus would endure that day. Then he was taken to Caiaphas, the high priest.

Under Jewish law, at least two or three witnesses were required before imposing a sentence of death. Similarly, Texas law says that testimony of an accomplice must be supported by other evidence in a capital crime. The Gospels tell us that the authorities solicited false testimony from many witnesses to ensure a fatal verdict against Jesus, although their testimony in the trial was often contradictory.

Caiaphas functioned as judge and prosecutor. He was intrigued

* Matthew 26:14–16
† Mark 14:37–43
‡ John 18:21

by the opportunity to question Jesus, who was well known for his sermons and miraculous healings. "I put you under oath before the living God, tell us if you are the Messiah, the Son of God,"* Caiaphas demanded. Jesus replied in the most inflammatory manner possible. He was innocent of the charge of blasphemy, he said, because he was indeed the Son of God. "I tell you, from now on you will see the Son of Man seated at the right hand of the Power, and coming on the clouds of heaven."†

"He has blasphemed!" Caiaphas shouted triumphantly, rending his clothes to add drama. "Why do we still need witnesses?"‡ When Caiaphas asked for the verdict, the jury of elders was unanimous: Jesus must die.

Before the crucifixion, however, Jesus was sent to yet another judge, Pontius Pilate, the Roman governor of Judea during the reign of Tiberius. Pilate was head of the judicial system and had the power to sanction executions. This was a Roman prerogative; the verdict of the elders was advisory. Pilate seemed to regard the case before him as a parochial matter with little evidentiary support. He irritably told the priests to take the matter into their own hands; he wanted nothing to do with it. But the priests pointed out that they didn't have the authority to execute condemned prisoners. Only Rome could do that.

A rebellion was stirring against the Roman occupation by Jewish peasantry who longed to restore the Kingdom of Israel. In Roman law, the concept of a Jewish king was a form of sedition. Pilate might have seen Jesus as a political actor who would best be put to death, serving as an example to other claimants to the throne. Rather than deny the charge, Jesus responded enigmatically, "My kingdom is not of this world."

* Matthew 26:63
† Matthew 26:64
‡ Mark 14:64

"Are you a king, then?"

"To this end I was born, and for this cause I came into the world, that I should bear witness to the truth."*

One can imagine that Pilate was hoping to evade responsibility for an execution he considered unfair, but instead of setting Jesus free, Pilate sent him to Herod Antipas (one of the sons of Herod the Great), who ruled over Galilee, Jesus's hometown, a center of revolutionary fervor. Herod had nominal authority to oversee the case, and he happened to be in Jerusalem for Passover. This additional judicial maneuver Osler likens to a federal writ of habeas corpus, which is the only way prisoners can appeal over the head of state authority.

Even before he set foot in Jerusalem, Jesus had been warned that Herod was intent on killing him. The two men would have known each other from Galilee, at least by reputation. Jesus had responded to the messenger, "Go and tell that fox for me, 'Listen, I am casting out demons and performing cures today and tomorrow, and on the third day I finish my work. Yet today, tomorrow, and the next day I must be on my way, because it is impossible for a prophet to be killed outside of Jerusalem.' "†

Herod was thrilled to have Jesus bound and brought into his presence, followed by scribes and priests who taunted the prisoner. As in a modern habeas hearing, the defendant had a high bar to overcome his original conviction. Moreover, Herod was angered by Jesus's bland responses, and he wasn't in the mood to resist the crowd. Herod ordered Jesus sent back to Pilate to carry out the sentence.

There was no more law to be sorted out. The final step in the legal journey of Jesus is akin to a clemency hearing. In Texas, the

* John 18:35–37
† Luke 13:31–34

equivalent role occupied by Pilate is the governor. Clemency was once common in Texas; Osler reports that before the U.S. Supreme Court overturned the death penalty in 1972, about 20% of condemned prisoners in Texas were granted freedom or had their sentences commuted. Since the restoration of the death penalty nearly six hundred prisoners have been executed in Texas (more than a third of the national total) and only three have been granted clemency. In 1993, a Texas case styled *Herrera v. Collins* argued that executing an innocent man would violate the Eighth Amendment to the Constitution, which prohibits cruel and unusual punishment. The U.S. Supreme Court ruled in the case that the purpose of federal habeas corpus is to address constitutional errors, not to relitigate the errors of the state proceedings, such as failure of the prosecution to disclose exculpatory evidence or of the defense counsel to provide adequate representation. William Rehnquist, the chief justice at the time, noted that, for innocent prisoners denied freedom, "under Texas law, [a] petitioner may file a request for executive clemency." He went on to sermonize, "Clemency is deeply rooted in our Anglo-Saxon tradition of law, and is the historic remedy for preventing miscarriages of justice where judicial process has been exhausted." Over to you, Governor.

Pontius Pilate faced similar political pressure as the governor of Texas when faced with an action that might be called mercy or justice but in either case was not going to be popular. Pilate was loath to stand against the mob excitedly awaiting the crucifixion, but he offered a compromise. During Passover, the Jews had a tradition of sparing the life of one prisoner. As it happened there were other crucifixions scheduled that day. One was a bandit named Barabbas, an insurrectionist with blood on his hands—exactly the kind of figure the Romans would like to extinguish. "Shall I release to you the King of the Jews?" Pilate beseeched the crowd. But the mob demanded that Barabbas be spared instead. "Why?" Pilate pleaded. "What evil has [Jesus] done?"

"Crucify him!" the crowd responded.*

The soldiers who guarded Pilate took the prisoner aside and stripped him and put a scarlet robe on him—scarlet being an insignia of royalty for the "King of the Jews." They made a crown of thorns and gave him a reed as a scepter. They blindfolded him, beat him, mocked him, and spat on him. In a final act of disgrace, Pilate himself flogged him, then turned him over to the crowd.

Jesus was offered wine mixed with myrrh to ease the pain, which he refused. Rather than being strapped to a gurney, as in modern-day Texas, his body was disabled when he was nailed to a cross. Death arrived when his strength gave out, his body slumped, compressing his lungs, and he died of suffocation.

Crucifixion was a public spectacle, as hangings once were in America. The last public execution in America took place in Owensboro, Kentucky, in 1936, when twenty thousand people came to witness the hanging of a young Black man, Rainey Bethea, who had been convicted of raping an elderly White woman. He was not convicted of killing her because murderers (although not rapists) were executed inside the state penitentiary, and the political establishment insisted on a public execution. However, sentiment against such displays had gathered to the point that Kentucky was the last state to sanction them, and the mob that showed up in Owensboro sensed that they might be witnessing the end of an era. An added attraction was the fact that the executioner would be a woman, Sheriff Florence Thompson, a widow with four children, who inherited the job after her husband, the elected sheriff, passed away. News reports describe thousands of gawkers arriving by car, wagon, and freight train, filling the hotels or sleeping in the vacant lot where the gallows had been erected. In the event, the

* Mark 15:12–14

sheriff delegated the actual hanging to a former cop who volunteered for the job.

But the death penalty continued to stir the national conscience, spurred in part by the repeated examples of horribly botched hangings—condemned prisoners writhing as they were slowly strangled in the noose when their neck failed to snap, or being decapitated if the fall was too lengthy. The search for a more humane form of execution led to electric chairs and gas chambers, which were touted as being more scientific and modern. They, too, were flawed. Witnesses were traumatized by the sight of heads catching fire by faulty electrocution, or prisoners moaning and gasping for breath in a gas chamber long after they were expected to have succumbed. Of all the means of executing, the firing squad was the most reliable.

In 2014, Austin Sarat, a professor at Amherst College, published "Gruesome Spectacles: Botched Executions and America's Death Penalty." He and a group of undergraduates examined the 8,776 capital punishments from 1900 to 2011. They found that 276 of them—over 3%—were flawed, often in grisly ways. In most states, including Texas, executions are now carried out by lethal injection. It sounds more humane—like dying in your sleep—but it has proved to be even more prone to catastrophic error. Seven percent of executions by lethal injection were botched because of untrained personnel, inability to find a suitable vein, or imperfect formulas for the deadly drug. In Texas, until 2009, the mortal concoction included three different drugs: an anesthetic and a paralyzing agent, intended to ease pain and prevent involuntary movements that would alarm the audience, followed by the lethal toxin. A local pharmacy would compound the formula. Texas has switched to a single dose of pentobarbital, a sedative, which in high doses causes death by respiratory arrest, like crucifixion.

Osler took the prosecution of Jesus to various cities and churches in America. In that first trial, in Waco, the congregation broke into juries of twelve. Most of the juries voted for life in prison—an option Jesus wasn't offered. "Of course, the jury pool was rigged at a church," Osler told me, "because the venire literally worshipped the defendant."

The largest religion in the world is built upon the injustice and suffering inflicted on Jesus. In a seminar I attended on Religion and the Death Penalty at the University of Texas School of Law, Osler pointed out that a large majority of people in death penalty states self-identify as Christians, which means that "without the support of Christians, we wouldn't have the death penalty."

The Theology of Execution

For centuries, the Catholic Church clung to the notion that civil authority to execute people superseded the Sixth Commandment, "Thou shalt not kill." The Old Testament is filled with capital offenses ordained by God, including magic, blasphemy, bestiality, adultery, incest, and violation of the sabbath. Saint Thomas Aquinas, a Dominican friar in the medieval period who became one of the most important theologians of the faith, wrote, "The life of certain pestiferous men is an impediment to the common good which is the concord of human society. Therefore, certain men must be removed by death from the society of men." But he added that execution can be allowed only when society itself would be damaged if not enforced.

Caiaphas, the high priest in Jerusalem, used that very argument to justify the execution of Jesus. "What are we to do?" the chief priests had asked him. "This man is performing many signs. If we let him go on like this, everyone will believe in him, and the Romans will come and destroy both our holy place and our nation." Caiaphas responded, "You know nothing at all! You do not understand that it is better for you to have one man die for the people than to have the whole nation destroyed."* Thus Jesus was condemned.

* John 11:49–50

Aquinas was writing during the Inquisition, when the church awarded to itself the power to combat heresy and witchcraft, among other sins, using torture to extract confessions and selling penances to people wealthy enough to avoid persecution. Once a confession had been obtained, the church turned the victim over to civil authorities to carry out the expected execution, much as the Jewish court turned Jesus over to the Roman governor, Pontius Pilate, demanding that Jesus be crucified.

In the twentieth century the church began to revise its teachings. Part of this was a defensive reaction to attacks on the church's firm stance against abortion; if Catholics believed in the sanctity of life from conception to death—"the womb to the tomb"—how could they support such a glaring contradiction? By the end of the millennium, the United States was practically alone among major Western nations for continuing to practice capital punishment. (Twenty-seven U.S. states have the penalty, but it is on hold in several of them. The federal government also maintains capital punishment. Under Donald Trump's first administration, thirteen prisoners were executed; none in the Biden administration.) American bishops campaigned to change the terms, saying that execution was wrong if nonlethal alternatives—such as life without parole—are available. However, a substantial majority of American Catholics still supports the death penalty, and within the church hierarchy there is resistance to surrendering execution as a punishment option. The Vatican's own penal code once called for executing anyone who attempted to kill the pope, although when John Paul II was shot in St. Peter's Square in 1981, he not only declined to pursue such punishment against his assailant, he forgave him and sought his pardon.

One of the prominent American voices on the issue of capital punishment was Cardinal Avery Dulles, who examined the controversy in the Catholic magazine *First Things*. He considered four principles the church relied upon in defending capital punishment.

At the top of the list was rehabilitation. Facing death, the convicted person may be motivated to repentance and conversion. The ladies on death row offer multiple examples of this. But if they have been rehabilitated, what purpose is served by killing them?

"Defense against the criminal" is the second of the church's arguments that Dulles addresses. Capital punishment certainly erases the threat of future harm, Dulles concedes, but life without parole also provides an effective defense for protecting society, the main reason death penalty sentences have declined.

If deterrence—the third argument—is to be effective, why not hold public executions instead of the private, invitation-only events where the condemned person is put to death as painlessly as possible? Why not chop off the head of the offender in a public square, as in Saudi Arabia, or hang them in front of the courthouse, as Texas used to do?

The final category, retribution, remains the strongest of the church's four arguments, at least in the United States. According to Saint Thomas, punishment in this life will spare the sinner in the next. But if society no longer buys the concept of the afterlife, capital punishment only serves to satisfy the vengefulness of society.

Cardinal Dulles acknowledges the weaknesses of these arguments. "The death penalty, we may conclude, has different values in relation to each of the four ends of punishment. It does not rehabilitate the criminal but may be an occasion for bringing about salutary repentance. It is an effective but rarely, if ever, a necessary means of defending society against the criminal. Whether it serves to deter others from similar crimes is a disputed question, difficult to settle. Its retributive value is impaired by lack of clarity about the role of the State. In general, then, capital punishment has some limited value but its necessity is open to doubt."

All of these arguments presume that the state carrying out the execution has been fair in its prosecution and that the condemned person is truly guilty of a crime worthy of death. The examples of these seven women on Texas death row pose a challenge to this presumption.

In Texas, the only crime eligible for the death penalty is capital murder. A murder becomes a capital murder under the following circumstances:

The victim is a police officer or firefighter acting in an official capacity.
The murder takes place during the commission of another felony, such as burglary or aggravated sexual assault.
The crime is a murder for hire.
The murder takes place during an escape from prison.
The killer is an inmate serving a life sentence.
The victim is a child under ten.
The victim is a judge killed in retaliation.
There are multiple victims.

How much greater than these crimes is the offense of executing an innocent person?

In 1995, Pope John Paul II rejected the use of capital punishment except "in cases of absolute necessity"—cracking open the door to abolition. Pope Francis, who had long opposed capital punishment, revised the catechism of the church in October 2020, declaring that the death penalty was "an attack on the inviolability and dignity of the person." Two years later he issued an encyclical, the highest form of papal communication, calling upon all Catholics to advocate for the end of capital punishment. "There can be no stepping back from this position," he declared. "Today we state clearly that 'the death penalty is inadmissible' and the church is firmly committed to calling for its abolition worldwide."

The only time Jesus faced the question of capital punishment, other than his own execution, he had been preaching in the temple when a scheming group of scribes and Pharisees brought before him a woman who had been caught in the act of adultery. What should we do with her, they asked. In the Torah, in Leviticus and Deuteronomy, the Law of Moses is clear: Adulterers should be put to death; however, because Jews did not have the right to administer capital punishment, they would be violating Roman law if they carried out the execution. If Jesus answered, "Stone her," he would be offending Rome; if he said, "Spare her," he would contradict Jewish teachings. Either answer would discredit his ministry and place him in peril.

"What do you say?" they asked.

Jesus stooped to the ground and wrote in the dirt. The Bible doesn't tell us what he was writing; perhaps he was just stalling. It's a startlingly interior moment in the life of a man who always had a ready answer or a parable that aptly shifts the moral argument. The scribes and Pharisees continued to hector Jesus until he stood and said, "Let him who is without sin among you be the first to throw a stone." Then he went back to scribbling in the dust. One by one the scribes and Pharisees walked away—itself a manner of confession—leaving the woman alone with Jesus. "Woman, where are they?" he asked. "Has no one condemned you?"

"No one, sir."

"Neither do I condemn you. Go your way and sin no more."*

* John 8:4–11

Last Chances

Sister Jeanne Thomas

The Final Appeal

JUNE 5, 2024, began with a three-judge panel at the Fifth Circuit Court of Appeals in New Orleans hearing the plea of Brittany Holberg—the last stop in the appeals process for most death-row inmates in Texas. For years, Brittany's case had been held up by the trial judge in Amarillo. "He's a good Christian man," the prosecutor, James Farren, said of the judge, "but he's personally opposed to the death penalty. So this writ lands on his desk, and until he rules on it, nothing can happen. If he rules against the state, we're going to appeal. If he rules against the defendant, then the defendant's going to appeal. But if he doesn't do anything, nobody else can do anything. So it sits on his desk for seven years." Eventually the trial judge was elected to a higher court and the new judge flipped the switch to start the process that led to that late spring morning in New Orleans.

Brittany was represented by David Abernethy, an appellate lawyer from Philadelphia who had never been involved in a death penalty case. He specializes in product liability. His firm, Faegre Drinker Biddle & Reath, had represented Brittany pro bono for about twenty years; two previous partners involved in her case had retired before Abernethy came to the plate.

The court is housed in a historic building, with marbled arches in the Italian Renaissance style, just off Lafayette Square in the French

Quarter. Many of the civil rights cases of the 1950s and 1960s were adjudicated in the dark, somber, wood-paneled courtroom where Abernethy stood.

"The jury that took eleven hours to sentence Brittany to die never heard that Ms. Holberg was exposed in utero to alcohol and hard drugs, born addicted, inconsolable, unable to tolerate being touched," he began. "They never heard that she was struck and shaken repeatedly as a young child." Abernethy described a childhood that targeted disaster. "She was raised in a drug den, where her parents cooked meth in a bathtub . . . raped repeatedly, beginning at age thirteen . . . gang raped, hospitalized, traumatized, wanting to die . . . severe cognitive impairments that were directly relevant to . . . how this homicide came to be committed."

Brittany's original trial attorneys had adopted a strategy of presenting her as a bright girl from a good family who had been accepted to Duke University; none of that was true. They chose to shield the jury from the horror of her life, believing that upright Amarillo citizens would be so appalled they would decide she was unredeemable. They chose to focus on the unlikelihood of future dangerousness rather than the lifelong traumas that created the shattered woman at the defense table. The prosecution countered by telling the jury Brittany had previously killed another old man, who in fact had died in hospice of pancreatic cancer. Then there was the testimony of Vickie Kirkpatrick, the jailhouse informant who had said that Brittany told her Towery's murder was "fun and amazing." The defense was not told that Kirkpatrick was a paid police informant, depending on that income to support her drug habit. She later repudiated her testimony. At the Fifth Circuit, Abernethy intended to paint a picture of a prosecutor willing to withhold or manufacture evidence to secure a death penalty.

One of the justices cut off that line of inquiry. Whether or not the jury had been told that Kirkpatrick was a paid snitch, the jury would still have learned about the "hammer, three forks, a butcher knife, a grapefruit knife, a cast iron skillet, and a steam iron," he observed, adding the clincher: "And he had a lamp shoved five inches down his throat." Abernethy focused on key elements of Kirkpatrick's disputed testimony—that Brittany had no remorse and had celebrated the killing—"which were, I submit, critically important to the jury's determination, not on the guilt of the homicide but on the sentence." It was Kirkpatrick's testimony that Brittany had stolen money from Towery that made it a capital crime, not just a gruesome homicide. These facts, Abernethy argued, were "powerful evidence for mercy, and if the jury had heard it, at least one of those twelve would have voted to spare her life."

The state responded that Kirkpatrick's testimony was irrelevant because it was followed by Brittany's own damning testimony when she was ill-prepared to do so. The prosecutor had taken her apart. "Holberg had to take the stand," one of the justices reasoned, "because someone else had just convicted her with her own words." If the state had disclosed the fact that Kirkpatrick had charges dropped in exchange for her testimony against Brittany, "Holberg may not have gotten slaughtered when she took the stand, because there would be no one saying this lady confessed to capital murder."

At an hour and twenty minutes, the justices retired from the bench to begin the monthslong deliberation on Brittany's fate.

~

There are several instances in Brittany's life that struck me as lost opportunities, moments when she might have been rescued from the tragic future that awaited her. "When I was a little girl I knew my real father's name was Jimmy Brogdon," she told me, "but that was all I knew about him other than that he did not want me." When Brittany was two, Brogdon was incarcerated, probably on drug charges. The following year her mother, Pamela, met John Schwartz, whom Brittany described as the biggest marijuana dealer in Amarillo. Pamela, a deputy in the Potter County Sheriff's Office, moved in with him. "She was a very broken human being who had never been taught how to love," Brittany recalls. "They continued their drug use my entire life."

Brittany described John Schwartz, her stepfather, as "my knight in shining armor." It was John who got Brittany to rehab on several occasions. Her real father, Brogdon, was in and out of jail or prison. He came to visit Brittany when she was four, although she doesn't remember much of that. The next occasion was when she was eleven. "I went to a movie with a friend. She and I were standing outside the theater in a strip mall in Amarillo. And I watched an old, beat-up car drive up to the curb." A man got out and walked past Brittany and her friends. "He was disheveled. He was dirty. But I couldn't quit staring at him. I just knew that was my dad." She followed him into a Payless shoe store and found him kneeling at the end of an aisle with a bunch of shoe boxes around him. She would later suppose that he intended to steal the shoes. She walked up to him and said, "Do you have a daughter?" He denied it, but then he said, "Birdie"—the nickname he had given her as a little girl. They spent three or four hours together as he introduced her to relatives she never knew she had. "After that, he took me back home and said that he would be back the next day, which was Easter, to take me to church and out to eat, and he never showed up."

When Brittany was sixteen and living with her boyfriend, Brogdon found her working in the Chess King clothing store. "It was one of those rare moments when I think he was sober." They went to dinner. "He just told me how very sorry he was for all the choices he had made," but he also suggested he had spared her a mountain of pain and disappointment by removing himself from her life. A few years later he was locked up again for heroin possession. By that time Brittany was on death row. There she got a lengthy letter from Brogdon. "I had never seen my father's handwriting," she recalled. On the back of the fourteenth page she found an outline of her father's hand. He told her to pay attention to a tiny ink dot in the center of his palm. He quoted Jesus to his disciples: "I tell you the truth, if you had faith even as small as a mustard seed, nothing would be impossible."*

When Brittany was seventeen and about to be married, she and her mother had an intimate conversation. Brittany felt safe enough to confess that the best friend of her stepfather had been molesting her for years, starting when she was twelve. Her mother responded, "That's okay. I slept with him too." Once, when Brittany was remanded to the Randall County Jail for a hearing, she was going through a box of affidavits and learned that her mother also had sex with Brittany's husband two weeks after their wedding. "I used to say with a mother like mine, a person needs no enemies," Brittany told me. "The sad truth is my mother hated herself and did what she did out of that hatred."

There was a moment that remains in some ways pure. It was after John Schwartz's sister, Karen, was murdered by her husband, and Brittany helped him clean up the blood. "This broke him in ways he never recovered from," but an unspoken bond between him and Brittany was forged in that experience. "He woke me up early one morning and told me to get dressed, he wanted to take me somewhere. I climbed on the back of his bike and we headed east on I-40 until he came to where he wanted to turn off." It was night but the stars lit the way. Rolling hills hid deep canyons that run like veins through the land. Georgia O'Keeffe taught school in this mystical locale. "My country," O'Keeffe wrote, "terrible winds and a wonderful emptiness." The red earth became the foundation of her palette.

Schwartz came to a roadside stop with a picnic bench. "As soon as we were off the bike he told me to follow him," Brittany says. He led her down a small trail of dirt and rock. She had no idea

* Matthew 17:20

where they were going. It was before dawn, and the path was black. "Finally we came to this huge rock and he stopped. He sat on the rock and patted the place next to him, so I climbed up and sat down.

"What I could not see was right in front of us, a tributary that led into the Palo Duro Canyon. After a while the sky began to lighten enough that I could really see. The canyon looked like a dark, never-ending hole. I remember looking at my dad and wondering why he had brought me here. He said, 'Just wait.' I do not know how long we waited, but when it happened it was one of the most unforgettable moments of my life. The sun began to crest over the opposite side of this winding and narrow canyon, and as it rose I watched the canyon turn from a dark hole into the most brilliant display of gold light you can imagine. It filled the canyon and painted the walls in the most amazing golden hue. Neither of us spoke, we just stared ahead, but I remember thinking, Only God can do this. I went back there alone many, many times during the deepest parts of my addiction. It took me a while to find it, but once I did it became my God spot."

~

When condemned inmates need medical attention, they are transported in a van to the University of Texas Medical Branch in Galveston, more than 250 miles from Gatesville. It's about a five-hour drive, longer if the driver and the guards break for lunch, while the prisoner remains in the back of the van, shackled, handcuffed, and locked in a cage—"very Hannibal Lecter–ish," Kimberly observed. When Melissa made the trip, she asked what would happen if they were in an accident; the one restraint she didn't have was a seat belt. "What difference does it make?" the officer replied. "Your sentence is to die."

I heard many tales of neglect in the old days of the prison, and some of the women remember them well. Erica had chronic dental problems, but according to her attorney, whenever she needed to see a dentist, he would simply extract a tooth or two, until the point when she had so few teeth she just had them all removed. For years she had to gum her food, much of which she couldn't eat. She had a chronic back problem that confined her to her cell because she wasn't allowed a walker. When she complained about the pain, she was told she needed to lose weight. With the changes in the prison administration she now has an impressive set of dentures, and after a relatively simple back operation, she can move about without pain. Both Kimberly Cargill and Sister Pia Maria were nurses in their past lives, so they had a common interest in medicine. They also had health problems; Kimberly had cardiac issues, and Sister Pia Maria hobbled about on a bad knee that needed to be replaced. Kimberly was shocked when the sister said she had to wait to find a benefactor to pay for the operation. "At least we, in prison, have access to healthcare," Kimberly observed.

Brittany received what is known as a "lay in" notice requiring her to travel to Galveston. She had no idea why. The officers were to pick her up early in the morning to get there for a noon appointment. They were slow to get out of Gatesville and didn't arrive in Galveston until after eight in the evening. The entire day Brittany had been bound and caged. She told the story to Sister Mary Guadalupe, who relayed it to me. "She was so hot and sweaty, in the back of this van, just soaking wet." When they arrived, two officers from Gatesville and a third from the hospital escorted her to the receptionist. She checked her records and told Brittany, "Oh, that's been taken care of. There's no need for you to be here."

Just as the officers were preparing to turn around and drive back to Gatesville, the officer from the hospital looked at Brittany, so wan and bedraggled, and asked the other officers if she had had anything to eat. She had not. He asked if he could get her a sandwich and a drink. Brittany assumed she was being taken to an isolation cell. But he deposited her in a room full of windows looking out on the Gulf of Mexico. Brittany burst into tears.

The Barbarian

THE SAME DAY David Abernethy was pleading for Brittany's life at the Fifth Circuit, she was assisting a celebration of Mass with Deacon Ronnie and a priest, Father Miguel Flores. It was warm—summer was announcing itself—and we all fanned ourselves with the liturgy bulletin as the women went into the hallway one by one for confession. Then the Mass began—a solemn Mass, with the "bells and smells," Ronnie gibed. When Father Miguel displayed the host—"Behold the Lamb of God"—Linda rang the bell, and again after communion. Taylor sang "Wayfaring Stranger" in a high, tentative voice. Erica supported her by singing quietly in her ear; Taylor had been very shy about singing, but the words resonated with these doomed women:

I'm just a poor wayfaring stranger
While traveling through this world of woe
But there's no sickness, toil, nor danger
In that bright world to which I go.

The nuns prostrated themselves in prayer, and then Father Miguel doused us all in holy water.

Afterward, I met up with the nuns at a steakhouse on the highway. Because of the sisters' poverty, restaurants were rarely a part of their life, and I sensed nervousness and excitement about being in a place that was ever so slightly taboo. The other diners regarded us with bemusement. I thought about how these women had been living the quietest life imaginable, silent and sequestered, but they had willingly plunged into a dark and complicated world, one that challenged them and sometimes frightened them but that filled them with purpose. And yet these same bold sisters were visibly out of place in a country steakhouse.

We talked about Deacon Ronnie, who had singlehandedly orchestrated this transformative encounter. I mentioned that, at the ceremony where the prison housing death row was renamed the O'Daniel Unit, Ronnie had sidled up to the top brass of the Texas corrections system and persuaded them that my article would be the best thing that ever happened to the prison system. Sister Mary Thomas laughed. "He persuaded us of that too."

"We consider him a saintly man," Sister Mary Guadalupe said. She compared Ronnie to Mother Teresa, in terms of being a slick operator. "She could get anything she wanted. He's like that."

There were four sisters with me; the prison had trimmed their delegation to three at a time, but Sister Mary Thomas had flown in from Parma, Italy, where she was serving as the general prioress of the order, and she was accorded the opportunity to join. She had visited the women on death row several times before and was touched by how much they remembered about her. "They'll ask me questions, like 'So how's your niece?' They had been praying for my niece."

When I pressed for more information about what the sisters learned at the Mass, they were coy. "Warm us up," Sister Mary Thomas suggested. "We'll open our hearts if you open yours."

This must be an old nun trick, I thought. I found myself talking to them about a troubling experience in my life that has since left me angry and frightened by the power of religion to destroy and deceive.

In 1980, a young preacher named Walker Railey came to the First Methodist Church in Dallas. The trauma of the JFK assassination had ebbed. Dallas itself was changing. It was still a conservative city, but a new humility had entered the culture; the response to the tragedy, and the humiliation that had fallen on the city because of it, awarded a dignity to Dallas that I would never have expected.

Railey was always aware that he was standing in Robert Goodrich's pulpit, but he immediately made it his own when he first came before the congregation and blew into the microphone, symbolically breathing new life into the church. Within a few years he was being called a "shining star of Methodism." He served as a liberal counterweight to the reactionary conservatism found in so many congregations in Dallas.

I saw Railey preach a midnight service one Christmas Eve. The church was packed. My wife, Roberta, and I were in the balcony, she on my lap. Since Goodrich departed, the church had been losing members for a decade, but Railey summoned a new audience who responded to his open progressivism, his advocacy for racial justice, and his learned sermons, polished and skillfully delivered. I watched his laser-blue eyes scan the sanctuary. It felt like he was searching for me. I suspect everyone there felt the same way, such was his charisma and allure.

Four months later, a few days after Easter, in April 1987, Railey's wife, Peggy, was strangled into a "persistent vegetative state" in their Lake Highlands home. We all thought that Railey was the real target of the attack. Walker had been working on a sermon at the Bridwell Library at SMU that night. When he came home, he found Peggy lying on the floor of the garage, convulsing, her face grotesquely discolored.

Was Dallas damned in some way to always having the brightest personalities extinguished by dark forces of bigotry and hate?

Railey's grieving staff recalled that he made a point of knowing the names of every one of the nearly six thousand members of the congregation, including the babies in the nursery. He had brought prestige back to First Church, and if his ambition reached further than that—well, he deserved what he sought, but why did he have to suffer such an awful test? It was always about Walker, the martyr, not Peggy, the victim.

Nine days later, Railey swallowed three bottles of tranquilizers and antidepressants, leaving behind a note that there was a "demon" inside him, and he was "the lowest of the low." The next morning police broke down his door to find that Railey had also fallen into a coma.

The police had been asking questions about the attack on Peggy. They learned that Walker had been having an affair with Goodrich's daughter, Lucy, who had changed her last name to Papillon. Before the attack, he had been receiving a series of threatening letters, which the FBI determined Railey had written himself. He was having trouble accounting for his whereabouts the night of the attack and neglected to mention that he had spent some of that fateful evening with Lucy. He seemed to have been constructing an alibi that night; for instance, calling his home answering machine, which didn't ring in the house, and leaving a message sometime after midnight that it was ten-thirty and he was headed home. Railey didn't have good answers for the detectives about what he was actually doing.

Being demon-possessed is not the same thing as confessing guilt; such theological language wouldn't convict him in court. When he finally woke up—as Peggy never would—he claimed to be innocent. When he testified before the grand jury, he took the Fifth forty-three times, but there was no indictment. The district attorney fecklessly suggested he leave town. In fact, Railey was already planning to run off to California with Lucy and leave his two young children behind. The police said that his five-year-old son, Ryan, had been partially strangled as well.

Texas Monthly asked me to investigate. From the beginning, I was having trouble controlling my behavior. Maybe all human stories, at least those touching upon questions of good and evil, cast a spiritual shadow, but this one turned me into someone I didn't recognize. The anger and despair inside me were boiling over in view of everyone I talked to. No doubt part of what upset me was the identity I felt with Railey; we were the same age; I had considered going into the ministry at one time, becoming a pastor very much like Walker Railey. Now I felt deceived by the whole religion enterprise; it was all a sham; we were pathetic dupes to have believed any of it. Hope for salvation, for "heaven," for divine forgiveness and justice—it was all bullshit. Nobody had done a better job of fooling us than Railey.

I spent many hours viewing videos of Railey's sermons. In one of them he wonders how the good people of society relate to the evil ones in their midst. "The Roman Empire didn't fall because of the barbarians outside the gates," he said. "It fell because it couldn't deal with the beastly people inside them." He suggested that there were barbarians all around us. "Who's the barbarian in your life this morning?" he asked. "Who could it be? Your husband? Your wife? Your neighbor? Your pastor?"

His sermons were full of such allusive clues. The term "barbarian" struck me because it suggested a category of human behavior that stood outside the axis of good and evil. It connoted a guiltlessness of a kind that could kill without remorse. Perhaps when he composed that sermon he was already planning to kill Peggy, but like so many amateurs he underestimated how hard it is to kill another person.

I was the last stop on Railey's exit tour before he departed for

California. I met him at his home in the Lake Highlands neighborhood of Dallas. The house was up for sale and had already been stripped of personal items. It was chilly and strangely humid, "like a mausoleum," Railey himself observed. Through church gossip he knew all about my spiritual turmoil. He also seemed to feel the same sense of identity with me as I did with him; several times he mentioned that he might become a journalist, now that the ministry was behind him. He had a way of guiding my questions so that they would be "tougher"—although the ground rules for the interview were that we wouldn't talk about Peggy's case or about Lucy. He told me he had been reading Psalms and playing golf—most recently with the legendary former district attorney Henry Wade (of *Roe v. Wade*). That was such a Dallas touch. I thought about the message Wade was sending to his protégés, who now ran that office and would determine whether Railey would face charges.

Railey showed me where he'd found Peggy convulsing on the concrete floor of the garage. Perhaps because of this mutual identity that we both seemed to feel, the conversation became more intimate than I had expected it to be, but he carefully avoided stepping over the line into confession. I asked about the demons he had referenced in his suicide note, but he slipped off into metaphors. "Depression—that's a demon," he said. "Low self-esteem." That's the denatured language of Methodism. What I really needed to hear from him was the dark spiritual journey he had taken into becoming a killer.

At the end of our interview, he wanted to know what I thought of him. "I think you're guilty," I said. I recounted the contradictions in his story, his evasiveness before the grand jury, the lies he told the police, his affair with Lucy. "I can't construct an innocent man out of that," I said.

"I hear what you're saying," he said, falling into his role as a pastoral counselor reflecting my feelings.

"Confess," I told him, "or it will haunt you forever."

"I am not guilty," he said. "I don't feel tormented by the guilt of what I didn't do."

A few days after our interview, he was in California, where he has continued to live.

It took Peggy twenty-four years to die. She sometimes cried or made noises, but it was impossible to know if they were purposeful, if there was still some trace of consciousness in her imprisoned brain.

Maybe Walker Railey is innocent; I can't know. He was finally tried in 1993, six years after the assault, in San Antonio. The jury said the prosecution failed to prove Railey's guilt beyond a reasonable doubt. He chose not to contest a civil trial, brought by Peggy's parents, who were awarded $18 million in damages. Railey declared bankruptcy and the settlement was set aside.

My father died in 2001. I wound up being the one to give his eulogy, in the same pulpit once graced by Robert Goodrich and later violated by Walker Railey. Even in that moment of my utmost grief, the sanctuary felt haunted. As I spoke, and wept, I thought about the loss of my father, and also of his faith. I will always wonder at the evidence of his last words: "Glorious! Glorious! Glorious!"

Radical Lives

From left to right, Sister Eva Nella, Sister Mary Guadalupe, Sister Jeanne Thomas, Sister Mary Thomas

At the steakhouse, Sister Eva Nella, from Mexico, reported on her conversation with Melissa, who told her that one of her sons was in the same prison with one of Erica's sons. Sister Mary Thomas said she had talked to Erica, who wanted to start some kind of program to show that women on death row can still be contributing members of society. "They get criticism for living off taxpayers' money and dragging it out." Sister Jeanne Thomas, the French prioress, added, "They want to show that maybe they have made a mistake—a big one—but they would perform this act of reparation to show they are reconciled with society. They want to bring into the world something positive." To me, these ideas were the product of isolation, a longing for relevance in a society that has forgotten about them, a society whose wrath they should be careful of awakening.

Sister Mary Guadalupe had tried to talk to Linda, but Linda held herself apart. I had much the same experience with Linda; she perseverated about her case in ways that seemed unrealistic. Sister Mary Guadalupe had a long talk with Brittany, who had heard from her lawyer that the decision from the Fifth Circuit could take as long as five months. "She said it was now in God's hands, you know, with the kind of abandonment she always has." Sister Mary Guadalupe paused and added, "I said to Brittany, you're a light to many people. And to us."

The nuns were all companionable women, set apart from the secular world by their garments and the air of sanctity that surrounded them. Sister Mary Thomas reminded me of a college friend who was similarly fair-skinned and blue-eyed. I wondered, if under that habit, she was also a redhead, although her brows suggested otherwise. I felt naughty even thinking about it.

I mentioned that I had recently learned more details about Darlie's case, which only added to the cloud of befuddlement surrounding her. The judge, Mark Stenson Tolle, had been on the verge of retirement when he was assigned the most sensational case in his undistinguished career. He transferred the trial to Kerrville, northwest of San Antonio, where the docket wasn't as crowded and he would be able to try it before his mandatory retirement.

If you were shopping for a death penalty jury, Kerrville would catch your eye, an ultraconservative community with a reputation for tough justice, but a woman accused of murdering her own children would be harshly examined in any jurisdiction. Deer season had just opened in Central Texas, which was an additional attraction for the lawyers. One of the prosecutors in the case was Toby Shook, who had been a few years behind me at Woodrow Wilson High School in East Dallas. He was facing Doug Mulder, Darlie's lead attorney. As a former prosecutor under Henry Wade, Mulder convicted an innocent man, Randall Dale Adams, of capital murder in 1977 for killing a Dallas police officer. (The conviction was overturned by the U.S. Supreme Court and was the basis of the documentary *The Thin Blue Line* by Errol Morris.) As a defense attorney, it was Mulder who'd persuaded a jury that there was insufficient evidence to convict Walker Railey.

Darlie had originally been awarded court-appointed attorneys. They had hired forensic experts who were confident the crime scene had not been staged, as police claimed; but her husband and mother decided to hire Mulder. He claimed that the original attorneys planned to implicate Darin in the killing, and he pledged he wouldn't do that. Indeed, no such evidence was produced in the trial. Darlie's conviction was one of Mulder's rare losses; he would blame it on the change of venue, but instead of preparing for the case, he had taken a Hawaiian vacation.

Judge Tolle retired as soon as Darlie's verdict was delivered, but the story had an appalling sequel. In 2008, the judge's daughter, Jeanmarie Geis, began falsely reporting threats against her life. Geis told police that she was being targeted because of Darlie's case, that it was payback for her father presiding over that trial. The police didn't believe her. And then she killed herself and her two children, completing the crime that perhaps Darlie had failed to do—if indeed she was guilty of killing her children and slitting her own throat. These cases were tangled in my mind; in some way they were the same crime, a reenactment of some monstrous human archetype.

"I don't know enough about human nature to parse all this," I admitted to the nuns.

"I don't like to reflect on why they did it," Sister Mary Thomas said. "If we focus on evil, we get sucked into it. Like that judge—he maybe cursed his own daughter. I don't know. But when you focus on evil, you become darker. So I don't try to understand why they did it or who did what. God sent us here to love them as they are—those who are repentant, those who are not, those who are in denial, those who are innocent."

"We just look at who they are now," Sister Jeanne Thomas added.

But a reporter has a different task.

Throughout this colloquy I noticed Sister Mary Guadalupe staring at me with a look that was either curious or skeptical. "Do you think you can give this story justice without putting the faith aspect into it?" she asked.

"That's the challenge, dealing with faith without being faithful," I admitted. I could admire a community of faith without believing the doctrine. I gave the example of the Mormons, who have developed a very caring and industrious culture that I admired. I had seen the work of Black Muslims in prison, who have been able to imbue discipline in inmates who previously had been so lost. In either example, their actual beliefs, which were bizarre, were beside the point; it was the community they created that mattered. I envied the fact that believers live in a world of meaning, even if their beliefs are delusory. A friend of mine, Lonnie Kliever, who was a scholar of religion at Southern Methodist University, spoke of religion as the frontier between creativity and lunacy. That seems especially true in America, where you can believe anything you want, and if you don't see it on the menu, you can cook up your own.

"Are you saying it's like a refuge, this belief system?" Sister Mary Guadalupe asked.

I replied that, in prison, faith gave the women an opportunity to change themselves, while they were also prevented from committing any more crimes. In my mind, faith on death row functioned like reform school, but one in which all the graduates are killed.

Sister Mary Guadalupe objected to my "reform school" comparison, which sounded to her as if faith was little more than a prescription for a healthy existence—"wake up in the morning, exercise, eat right." That wasn't what had transformed the women on death row. "This is beyond that, beyond even their relationship with each other. I'm not saying all of them see it that way, but for those who have the capacity to do so, it's not a *discipline*."

Sister Mary Thomas added, "We wouldn't offer our whole lives—in virginity, poverty, and obedience—to a *discipline*. It wouldn't give us joy and the capacity to live together, connecting cultures and languages and education backgrounds. That wouldn't explain the capacity we have to—"

"To allow you to live a *radical* life," I said, teasing her with that favorite word of hers.

"I used the wrong word with you," she laughed. "My desire initially was for God. And within that desire, I wanted my love for God to be radical. So it wasn't like I had started to be radical and then latched on to religion."

She was still chewing on my suggestion that oblature might have been a smart political move. Referring to the women on the row who had taken on that challenge, she admitted, "Perhaps it's more helpful to their cause to be faithful Christians and to have repented—you could look at it from that perspective. Maybe that's good for your story, to have this contrast with us, since we're not gaining anything from religion, but we're giving up a lot. What we're gaining is the joy of our friendship with Christ."

I wasn't sure how to evaluate the worthiness of religion in the way Sister Mary Thomas framed it. Certainly they paid a great price for their faith, and their sacrifice was noble and beautiful in its way—as was true of the women on the row. They all lived in an atmosphere that was beyond me. Religion offered consolation, no doubt; and as I immersed myself in the belief of these women, I was reminded of the spiritual wisdom of Jesus's teachings, which were marvelous even without the promise of eternal life in heaven. Were I to ally myself with the faith of these women, my biggest sacrifice would be of reason. That said, reason alone doesn't explain the glories of existence, the beauties of the natural world, the splendid mysteries we accept without a second thought. And so I find myself suspended, my mind holding me apart from belief and my heart swollen with gratitude for the life I have enjoyed.

The waiter came around for the third time to see if we were going to order anything besides Diet Coke and Arnold Palmers. The sisters claimed they weren't interested in ordering, which made me sad. I hated to see them pass up the opportunity. "At least some french fries," I suggested. If I hadn't dined out since I was a teenager, that would have been my choice.

"Onion rings," Sister Mary Thomas said, her eyes bright with excitement.

Marilyn's Ghost

"Justice"

My examination of the seven condemned women profoundly changed my opinion about the way justice is administered in Texas, and probably anywhere in America. I now see the law as a kind of board game, in which risk and randomness are at play.

Each of the seven had drawn the Woman card, which had its advantages and liabilities, especially in the world of criminal law, which is overwhelmingly male. A woman facing prosecution for a violent offense is more likely to be seen sympathetically by a jury or thought to be less capable of murder in its various degrees; therefore, prosecutors seeking to obtain a death penalty will attempt to destroy the femininity of the defendant—she must be turned into a monster. The fact that Brittany's crime was so gruesome made it easy to demonize her, but James Farren, the prosecutor, still thought it necessary to use a jailhouse informant, who was rewarded for her testimony, to elevate a homicide into a capital murder. To demonstrate future dangerousness, he also falsely suggested Brittany had killed before. She may be guilty of the murder she was tried for, but what if she was not? These same underhanded techniques could also put an innocent person on death row.

Women are judged by different moral standards. Darlie, the suburban housewife, was painted as superficial and immoral, although her husband shared the same values and he was not considered a suspect. Darlie's affect and behavior after the death of her sons struck the jurors as insufficiently bereft, but suppose Darin had been the one spraying Silly String on his murdered sons' grave. Would that have made the impression on the jurors that Darlie did?

Women facing capital murder charges rarely have a history of extreme violence. That's one of the reasons there are so few women on death row; prosecutors must convince a jury that the accused will kill again, often a difficult case to make. Sandra Babcock, a clinical professor of law at Cornell University, has studied the prosecution of women who wound up on death row. There are certain commonalities: 85% were mothers at the time of their arrest; 96% were survivors of gender-based violence; 80% experienced intellectual or physical disabilities; and 90% had no prior violent convictions. Each of these factors described Melissa. To persuade a jury that a woman with this history deserves to die poses a challenge. A prosecutor must shake the preconceived notions—especially in Texas—that women are inherently nonviolent. Babcock calls this process "defeminization." She argues, "They manufacture evidence that is designed to shred the image the jury has, that this is a woman who is vulnerable, who has experiences that put her on this pathway that she otherwise would not have gone down. What they're trying to do is show that she's intrinsically evil." Babcock used the example of Melissa and her husband. The authorities grilled Melissa for hours, demanding to know what she fed her kids and how she cared for them. "When they interrogated her partner, the only mention of the children was when the cop said, Oh, I see you have a whole bunch of kids. Wow, that must be tough. I'm a dad, too, you know?"

With Melissa, who presents herself as passive, whose face and bearing reflect a lifetime of battering and sexual abuse, the prosecutor attacked her fertility. If she got pregnant in prison, he warned, she would have access to the prison nursery—more victims—

brushing aside the implication that, in the unlikely event she got pregnant, she would have to have been raped by a prison official.

The Color card was drawn by three of the seven: Melissa is the only Hispanic woman in history on Texas death row; Erica and Linda are Black. As of this writing, there are 161 men on death row, the lowest number since 1985; about three-quarters of them are Black or Hispanic. When you look at Harris County alone, twenty of the last twenty-one people sentenced to death are Black or Hispanic.

The Venue card often determines whether an offender lives or dies. Kimberly was tried in Tyler, a highly religious town in the Bible Belt. Kimberly's sister described her to the jury as "the devil." Such language rings in the ears of conservative Christians. "I don't think that she was convicted of murder or sentenced to death for murder," Kimberly's lawyer, Kathrin Schwesinger, told me. "It ended up being a death penalty case because Kimberly had some bad acts in her history, some bad acts regarding children. And she had the misfortune of all this happening in Tyler, Texas."

C. F. Hazlewood expects several women will get execution dates soon; in his opinion, the most likely are the two sentenced in Harris County, Linda and Erica, where there is a backlog of death penalty convictions. "They're gonna try to clean out death row, male and female," he predicts. "Smith County"—where Kimberly was convicted—"is pretty aggressive." He adds: "Taylor's toast. Bowie County is gonna kill you, that's all there is to it."

Perhaps the cruelest card to draw in this game is Class. Most of the women on the row were initially represented by appointed lawyers. Public defenders are exalted for their selflessness, but in fact court appointments can be a money mill. Before 2001, when the Fair Defense Act provided federally funded public defenders, representation in Texas was typically supplied by friends of the judge. That's still the case in many places in Texas, especially at the initial appeal level. "A lot of these lawyers were appointed because they would move the cases quickly and cheaply," Jim Marcus, the co-director of the Capital Punishment Clinic at the University of Texas, told me. Most of the women on death row were convicted in an era when appointed lawyers were given a flat fee—$30,000 would be typical—for the trial, and perhaps $5,000 or $10,000 for an investigation that, properly done, might run into the hundreds of thousands.

At times, Kimberly's defense attorney seemed to be working against his client. He elicited testimony from his own forensic psychologist that Kimbery met the criteria for being a psychopath or sociopath—a powerful indictment when it came time for the jury to consider future dangerousness. In Linda's case, the attorney the court assigned was Jerry Guerinot; he had represented more than thirty capital murder cases and lost them all. Twenty-one of his clients received the death penalty and ten have been executed so far. By appointing Guerinot, the court essentially condemned Linda before her trial. Linda has described Guerinot as "an undertaker for the State of Texas." (Guerinot explained his record by claiming he had always been given the hardest cases. He is no longer representing clients facing a possible capital murder charge.)

The ingrained resistance to statewide judicial standards in Texas is reflected in the 254 counties, each with their own ways of doing business. Austin, in Travis County, is the most progressive city in Texas, but until 2019 it was also the largest city in the country without a public defender office. Judges still have a choice in appointing a defense attorney for an indigent client, and may prefer to have someone they know in their courtroom rather than a public defender. Many parts of the state don't have highly skilled criminal defense lawyers to draw upon, which guarantees inexperienced counsel.

"When I was graduating from law school in Houston, I was looking around for jobs, and I asked people, 'How do you become a criminal defense lawyer?'" Marcus recalls. "They said, 'Go down to the courthouse and make contributions, and the judges will start giving you cases.' Nobody thought there was anything wrong with it." He pointed to Harris County, where court-appointed attorneys can still make as much as a million dollars a year representing indigent clients by taking on unmanageable caseloads. Given her representation, Linda Carty never stood a chance, nor did Melissa, who fell victim to a justice system that was itself a criminal enterprise. She then became ensnared by an appeals process that was ready to kill her to avoid addressing the corruption that had led to her conviction. In Texas, at least, we should have a word other than "justice" for a system so profoundly flawed.

Erica

Erica Sheppard

Abuse is a common thread among women who commit violent crimes, but the life of Erica Sheppard stands out as one of unremitting cruelty. She was born in Bay City, in the rice fields of South Texas. Her childhood was divided between life with her mother, Madelyn Johnson, in Houston, and her maternal grandmother, Annie Lee Smith, in Markham, a speck of a town just down the road from Bay City. Her mother testified that Erica's father was an abusive alcoholic. Madelyn had a series of lesbian lovers, some of whom abused Erica and her older brother, Jonathan. Madelyn personally disciplined her children with a leather belt and switches from a plum tree. After she tried to strangle Erica with a telephone cord, Erica took temporary refuge in a youth shelter.

When Erica was a young child, Madelyn sometimes left her children in the care of a sadist nicknamed Cookie. "I was about seven and Erica was about five years old," Jonathan testified in an affidavit. "It would have been the summer before Erica entered kindergarten. It was the worst summer of my life." Cookie abused the children nearly every day—slapping, whipping, forcing them to walk to the store barefoot. "We would burn our feet on the pavement," Jonathan remembered. "One day, I accidently spilled a Kool-Aid drink on the kitchen floor. Cookie became angry and made me get on my hands and knees and lick it up off the floor. I remember being very scared and crying . . . I recall this incident very distinctly, and it still makes me emotional to think about it."

Cookie had a boyfriend, whose name Jonathan couldn't recall. "Cookie would make my sister perform oral sex on this man . . . Cookie would make me sit there and watch. It happened several times that summer. I do not know what other sexual acts Erica was made to perform on this man. But I recall feeling very bad at having to watch my little sister go through this."

Jonathan finally told his grandmother what was happening. "I recall overhearing my grandmother and my mother arguing about it. My mother told my grandmother that we were lying and, as a result, my mother never reported the abuse to the authorities." But after that, the children went to live with their grandmother.

Erica failed the fourth grade. She dropped out of school in the tenth grade. She had her first abortion at thirteen. She was repeatedly raped from the time she was a child until her arrest, and she bore three children by different fathers. Multiple beatings had led to brain damage. Later, when Erica's husband beat her and repeatedly threatened her with a gun, she went to the police and got a protective order, but then she went back to him. As in Brittany's case, Erica's jury heard very little of her background, because the judge sided with the prosecution in withholding such testimony and then allowed the prosecutor to claim that there was "no proof" Erica had ever been abused. Erica had hoped to become a nurse, but her past blocked the path to that future.

In June 1993, less than a month before all the tragedies in Erica's life culminated in a final apocalypse, she took a bus from Bay City to Houston, where Jonathan was living. Erica and Jonathan had never been close, perhaps because of the guilt and shame each of them carried. She asked Jonathan if she and her baby could stay with him. She was fleeing her husband, Jerry Bryant Jr., who had abused her habitually, once knocking her unconscious in a hospital parking lot when she was attending her infant daughter.

Jonathan was in a relationship with a White man named James Dickerson. Erica and Dickerson were both nineteen. Soon after Erica moved in, the two of them had a conversation while he peeled potatoes. He said he was tired of not having any money. He couldn't even order pizza. He was thinking about going back to the "gangster life." Another friend of Jonathan's, Korey Jordan, age sixteen, was in the apartment and overheard the conversation. Dickerson and Erica began talking about stealing a car. They both knew it could be a fateful encounter. Jordan testified he heard Dickerson say, "If taking a life is what I have to do to get some money, then that's what I have to do." Erica responded that the ideal victim was "a skinny White woman walking between her car and her apartment with no children." They decided to strike that very night. They put on dark clothes and spotted a woman fitting their target in the same complex, but the woman suspected something and ran into her apartment before they could get to her.

The next night the plotters tried again. Erica and Dickerson broke into an apartment belonging to Marilyn Sage Meagher, a popular real-estate agent in Houston. The object was to steal her car, but it turned into another wildly incompetent homicide so characteristic of the murders represented on death row.

Kelley and John

On June 30, 1993, Kelley Meagher came home from work around six in the evening. She lived with her mother in a townhouse in Houston. Kelley was part of a large Irish Catholic clan; her mom, Marilyn Sage Meagher, had seven siblings, and most of them lived in Houston. Kelley noticed that her mother's car was missing, but that wasn't unusual. She unlocked the gate that led to a small entryway and went inside.

Tall, with long brown hair, wide-set blue eyes, jutting chin, and a wide smile like her mother's, Kelley always had a job. She had just graduated from high school and was working in an office while taking classes at a junior college before going to Louisiana State University in the fall. "The Sages work hard and don't give up" was the family mantra, although since Marilyn's divorce they never made enough money to be comfortable. Kelley kicked off her shoes and got some leftover pasta from the refrigerator, which Marilyn had brought home from work the day before. Marilyn was a real-estate agent in Houston for more than a decade but had taken an extra job in the evenings as a hostess in an upscale Italian restaurant. Sometimes Marilyn couldn't pay the utilities, so they ate by candlelight, but she made it fun somehow. She was proudly supporting a son, Michael, in college, and Kelley would be going to LSU in a few weeks.

On that day there was tension in the family because of a quarrel between Marilyn and one of her sisters, so Kelley called her grandmother, Margaret O'Connor Sage, the indomitable matriarch of the Sage clan, to fill her in. The extended family had clung together through many tragedies—accidents, cancer, disabilities, failed marriages, spiritual crises—but this quarrel between siblings was cause for alarm.

When she hung up the phone, Kelley headed back to her older brother's room, which had been given over to the television since he went off to college. It was dark in the hallway, and Kelley stubbed her foot into what felt like a pile of laundry. Then she felt something soaking through her pantyhose and instantly realized it was blood.

She went back into the kitchen.

"I remember thinking, Okay, she's been hurt. I knew it was her, and I knew there was blood." She hit redial and tried to explain to her grandmother what had happened but she couldn't make herself clear, and then it occurred to her that she should be calling 911 instead, so she called, and the first thing the operator asked was, "Is she breathing?" The operator asked again but Kelley couldn't do it, she couldn't go back there. She asked a neighbor to come in and look.

Suddenly the street was full of emergency vehicles. Television crews arrived. Friends and strangers gathered on the little dead-end street. The detectives grilled her. Was the gate locked or not? "I remember being asked that like eight hundred times." She didn't know. She had put the key in the lock as usual and turned it, but did it click? "They wanted me to be able to know that, and I remember thinking, I can't know that." She was standing in the street, no shoes; somewhere along the line she had removed her bloody pantyhose. She was eighteen years old and would never have a mother again.

Kelley spent the next couple nights with her father. She spoke to the cops and the district attorney, who were still trying to find out if the assailant was someone Marilyn knew, but Kelley was certain that the murder wasn't personal. Her mother was beloved. She was beautiful; she had a zany side, and she loved to dance to country-western music. She hadn't had a boyfriend for several years. Whoever killed her didn't seek revenge. Nobody hated her.

More than a thousand friends showed up for the funeral at St. Michael the Archangel Catholic Church on the Fourth of July weekend, spilling into the aisles, standing in the back. People passing by asked if some political figure had died. Kelley had prepared a poem that she read at the service.

No experience will ever be the same,
Without her there to share the joys and pain.
I thought my life had just begun,
Now all I see is a setting sun.

Shortly before the mourners gathered in Houston, the police arrested Erica Sheppard and James Dickerson at the Economy Motel in Bay City, Erica's hometown. Korey Jordan had notified police about what he had overheard. Dickerson soon confessed.

When Kelley was allowed back in the apartment to gather some clothes, her uncle John Sage went with her. "She was in a terrible state," he recalled. The place hadn't been fully cleaned yet and he saw Kelley's bloody footprints in the hall. One of the cops told him that Erica and Dickerson had gone into the apartment armed with a paring knife—the one they had used to peel potatoes. Their goal was to steal a car so they could drive to Bay City. They demanded the keys. Marilyn started screaming and threw thirteen dollars at them, saying, "Here's my money but I'll keep my car." It was a fatal act of bravado. The car they stole, a Mazda sedan, was the first Marilyn had ever bought new.

John was Marilyn's big brother and Kelley's favorite uncle. Of the eight siblings, John and Marilyn were the closest, just a year apart in high school, St. Thomas for John and St. Agnes for Marilyn. She was always getting in trouble with the nuns for her silly antics, like wearing crazy socks that mocked the dress code. They both went to LSU, where John played football, becoming an all-conference defensive tackle. They shared a car, and each week John would leave his dirty clothes in the trunk and Marilyn would return them clean and folded.

One of the detectives told John, "I've investigated homicides for twenty-five years, and I've never seen anything this brutal." John pressed him for details. Erica's brother Jonathan—Dickerson's lover—lived in the same complex. The killers saw Marilyn unloading some items from the trunk, and when she went inside, they followed. Up to this point, the crime was unfolding just as Erica envisioned.

Dickerson held Marilyn down and tried to slit her throat, but the paring knife was too dull, so he told Erica to fetch a butcher knife. She brought an assortment of knives from the kitchen. They used at least three of them, the biggest one was used to stab Marilyn in the neck, severing the jugular and lodging in her vertebrae. The medical examiner said that the killing blow was so forceful that it might have been delivered by two people. Like Karla Faye Tucker and Brittany Holberg, Erica and her accomplice were spooked by the death rattle and continued their attack after Marilyn was dead, putting a plastic bag over her head to silence her. A ten-pound statue of a mother and child was used to smash Marilyn's head. The statue broke in half. When John saw his sister's body in the casket, he was wrecked by the sight of her wounds.

Erica and Dickerson each accused the other of doing the actual killing, but in Texas it wouldn't matter; the accomplice is just as guilty as the killer. Kelley testified in both trials. She was struck by the difference in the demeanor of the defendants. Dickerson, tried first, was hunched and remorseful; he was already diagnosed with HIV, and AIDS would kill him before the state had a chance. Erica seemed defiant, passing notes, giggling at times. "It was just bizarre," Kelley recalled. "One might think she bought tickets to the wrong movie."

Marilyn's family was passionately divided over the death penalty. Some of the Sage siblings wanted Erica to die, and others didn't want her blood on their hands. Life without parole wasn't an option then. They finally compromised by requesting that Erica not be executed but that she remain on death row.

Kelley mentally withdrew from that conversation. The murder was tragic, but the animosity was pointless, steam from a boiling kettle. "I didn't want it to eat my life," Kelley told me. She was nonetheless plagued by depression and nightmares. On her junior year abroad, in Spain, some friends took her to a Brad Pitt movie; she went without knowing what it was about. *Seven* is a terrifying film about a serial killer. Kelley was trapped in the middle of the row in the theater. The images affected her sleep for days. She still monitors what she exposes herself to.

John was at the bottom of a deep well of depression. He couldn't sleep. He suffered panic attacks. He quit his job and filed for a psychological disability—a terrible blow to this proud man, who had been a football hero and a millionaire real-estate investor. Helplessness had not been a part of his nature until then.

During Dickerson's trial, while the prosecutor played a tape of his graphic confession, John looked at this young man and saw a freshly barbered monster wearing a new suit. He kept visualizing putting his hands around Dickerson's neck. John was a powerful man; it would be so easy, over in a moment, not like what they did to Marilyn. Erica's trial was a year later, but John couldn't imagine killing her. Maybe it was because she was a woman; he felt only overwhelming sadness when he looked at her. "I was distraught. You just come to a real dark place and face evil square in the eye."

After Erica and Dickerson were sent away to prison, John realized he was in a kind of spiritual prison himself. During one sleepless night he went into the bathroom and saw himself in the mirror, haggard, unshaven, with bloodshot eyes, his shoulders slumped. He began to weep. Humbled by grief and confusion, he fell to his knees and prayed. "God, I can't go on like this," he said. "Tell me what to do."

A voice seemed to answer: "Give it to me, John."

He had never been much of a reader but he turned to Catholic theologians, especially Thomas Merton and Henri Nouwen. His spiritual journey led him to work with the Sycamore Tree Project, an international volunteer organization that brings together offenders and victims (although not the victims of their own crimes), with the goal of creating accountability. John was moved by the program but frustrated that it was not reaching enough prisoners, so in 1998 he decided to start his own organization, Bridges to Life. Every Monday night he would drive to a prison in Beaumont. He was surprised by the number of victims who wanted to join the experience and by how many prisoners volunteered for the program. That first year he graduated forty-one inmates. Now Bridges to Life is in more than two hundred prisons and almost a hundred thousand men and women have successfully passed through the program. Unlike most prison fellowships, Bridges to Life requires inmates to admit to their crime of record.

John has come to believe in redemption. "I wouldn't do the work I do if I didn't believe that someone could change significantly. I've seen them change. I have seen them get out and do well. I think their hearts can change." As for himself, he says, "My journey went to another level. It's more about forgiveness."

All these years John has longed to meet Erica. The prison system operates a mediation program, and he harbored the hope that, if they could talk, she would take some meaningful level of responsi-

Kelley Meagher

John Sage

bility for the killing. He wanted to tell her directly about the damage she had wreaked on the lives of Marilyn's family and friends, and the hurtful legacy that has been passed to new generations. Erica claimed to be interested in meeting, but she set terms that violated prison protocols. Prison officials indicated to John that the meeting wouldn't give him the closure he was looking for anyway.

Twenty years after Marilyn's murder, John was making a presentation about Bridges to Life to the warden of the O'Daniel Unit. John knew that the victim of a crime typically cannot enter a unit that houses the offender. "Would you just *show* me the building where death row is?" he asked the warden. Even this felt like he was bending the rules. To his surprise the warden walked him directly into the unit and to the command-center desk just outside the row. John hadn't expected to get this close.

"Well, what do you want to do?" the warden asked him.

"If you would just walk me around there, let me look at her, I promise I won't say anything inappropriate."

An officer unlocked the barred gate. John's heart began to thump. He was feeling powerful emotions that were hard to describe. He had no trouble recognizing Erica, although she was older now and had put on weight. He paused in front of her cell. What struck him was how dark it was; the window was covered by a piece of cardboard; the space was little bigger than a double closet. Erica stood and held on to the bars. "I didn't say a word," John recalls. "Just looked at her. I thought it was sad. I looked at her hands and thought, These are the hands that helped murder my sister. But if you had told me I could do whatever I wanted to her, I had no need to retaliate. She cleared her throat, kinda coughed. It was only a matter of seconds. And then I walked out. For me, that was the last little piece of forgiveness."

Kelley Meagher Watts, who is now a practicing psychologist in Houston, passes near the murder site nearly every day. She had been living in New York but eventually decided to return to Houston and get a doctorate in psychology. Unlike her uncle John, she didn't have questions for Erica to answer. She already knew as much as she needed.

John had asked if she would *go* into the prisons and testify for Bridges to Life. Kelley was reluctant, but she would do anything to support him. "My task was to make them feel the human consequence" of their actions, so she painted a picture of her relationship with her mother and described the loss of Marilyn being in her life. The prisoners asked probing questions, they really wanted to know details. She described the nightmares, the struggle to keep from being defined by the crime. Outside of prison, if she shared her past with someone, she worried that they couldn't handle the intensity. And yet people knew. Somehow her reputation as a victim preceded her. "No one in my circle ever had anything happen like this," she told the prisoners. "So the isolation was very strong."

She and I talked about the question of evil. When Kelley hears the word "evil," "the hair on my neck goes up because I always feel like it's propaganda, like it's used in a very manipulative way to evoke emotional, impulsive, rash actions." As a mental health professional, she finds other terms to explain human behavior. "It serves me well to believe that generally humans are good," she said. "It's not that I don't believe in evil at all. I think it's overused. We justify a lot of stuff when we write someone off as 'evil.'" It affects how people feel about the death penalty, she said. "Think about what you would vote for, if you consider all the people on death row and have decided that they're evil, versus what you would vote for if you think these are people with flagrant mental health issues and probably a lot of complex trauma. I think we must be very careful with that language."

"How do you fit grief into that thinking?" I asked her. Grief and anger were so tied together in John's journey, which had been focused on the killers. "There's just no space for them in my grief," Kelley said. "I officially uninvited them to my future way back, probably right after it happened."

I asked if, like John, she had come to forgive Erica. We were sitting in her breakfast nook. The house was decorated for Halloween, with Day of the Dead skulls and skeletons. "I remember getting in the car with Johnny after I told my story in prison the first time, and I had been asked that question about forgiveness. I told him I disappointed the audience, because here were these men that really want to be forgiven. My honest take was I didn't feel it was mine to forgive."

"Explain that," I said.

"It happened to me, but it wasn't done to me. I never identified with the idea of being a victim. Erica took the life of my mother, but it wasn't personal. She would have taken anybody's life that got in the way of her and her ride to Bay City."

John Sage called me, wanting to make sure I hadn't called him an "All American" football player, as it said on his certificate. Officially, he was a second-team All American, so I changed it to all-conference in the SEC. Then he said he had something else he wanted me to know.

"Six days after Marilyn was murdered, I believe I had a spiritual visit from her." It was very physical, he said. His wife, Frances, thought he was having a heart attack.

He hadn't been sleeping more than two hours a night. He was lying in bed, "and I started seeing this kind of light going around the corners of the ceiling, all the way around the room in a circular, counterclockwise fashion. At first I thought it was some lights coming through the window, but the shutters were closed. I even looked to see if there was anything out there. Then it sped up into a smaller, kind of elliptical form, and hovered above the foot of the bed about five feet high. And it got faster and faster and suddenly Marilyn's face, from the neck up, was there. And I've never seen any human being look that beautiful, that flawless. She's a beautiful woman, but this was beyond anything I've ever seen. She hovered there, and then she said, 'Thank you.' And I just impulsively reached out with one of my arms, and that light came through my right arm and out my left leg, and my body raised up. My left leg raised up at about a forty-five-degree angle, and I was shaking. My wife woke up and said, 'What's the matter?' Then it just went away."

In the Garden

I USED TO believe that, if there were justice in Texas, Walker Railey would be on death row. I don't feel that way now. Neither Texas nor any other state has the moral authority to administer the final punishment. Railey enjoyed the presumption of innocence that is awarded mainly to powerful, well-off, White men. If he fit the racial and class demographic of most prisoners in Texas, he likely would have been executed by now. Instead, I recently got a Facebook suggestion to reconnect with him. Walker Railey has nearly eight hundred Facebook friends.

As I write, Melissa Lucio is still on death row, more than three years after the Court of Criminal Appeals stayed her execution. In April 2024, a district judge in Cameron County, Arturo Nelson, who presided over Melissa Lucio's trial, recommended that her conviction be overturned. Both Vanessa Potkin, who represents Melissa with the Innocence Project, and Luis Saenz, the district attorney in Cameron County who had been so reluctant to deal with the Texas legislators, acknowledged that the prosecution had withheld exculpatory evidence in the trial. This is an exceedingly rare event. After the CCA failed to act, Judge Nelson took the extra step of declaring, in October 2024, that Melissa was "actually innocent" in response to evidence amassed by her legal team.

(Among other considerations, the medical examiner had inaccurately claimed that Mariah's bruises were inconsistent with a fall.)

Only two women have left death row alive. Cathy Henderson had spent nearly two decades in Gatesville and was granted a new trial. She pled guilty to murdering a three-year-old boy she was babysitting in 1994 and was sentenced to twenty-five years in prison. She died two months after her plea. Pam Perillo spent the first twenty years on death row for two murders; in 2000, she was resentenced to life in prison; twenty years after that she was freed on parole. The world had changed in the forty years she'd spent behind bars. She was confounded by the microwave and television remote control. She changed her name and moved to the country.

I asked Melissa what she was going to do if and when she finally gets out. If she is found to have been unjustly imprisoned, she will be eligible for compensation from the state—a lump sum of $80,000 per year served, plus an annuity based on life expectancy. There's a private camp for women leaving prison that helps them adjust to freedom. Melissa hopes to go there. "One thing for sure—I'll never wear white again."

Time is running out for the other condemned women, all of whom are in a state of purgatory. Erica, Linda, Kimberly, Darlie, and Brittany could each receive a date soon. Only Taylor has more appeals ahead of her. She may one day have the row to herself. There are still more than two thousand people on death row in the United States, including forty-seven women.

I never became religious in the way that Deacon Ronnie and the nuns and the condemned women all prayed for. I was grateful for their thoughtfulness. I do sometimes pray, but it's always the same prayer, following the wisdom of Meister Eckhart, the medieval Catholic theologian: "If the only prayer you ever say in your entire life is thank you, it will be enough."

Brittany recalled the moment when Deacon Ronnie first broached the subject of inviting the nuns into the prisoners' lives, explaining that they were also confined with a small group of women in rooms they called cells, and their day-to-day activities were very similar to those of the prisoners. "That honestly seemed inconceivable," Brittany wrote me. Over time, she says, the nuns helped them learn how to live better in community. "They have showed us how to approach each other with more humility and grace simply by being an example of this themselves. They have shared with us their beautiful ways of addressing everyday issues with one another." Before the nuns began their ministry in Gatesville, "there were struggles," Brittany noted. "Spending time with the sisters gave us a blueprint of sorts as to how we could better handle things and cover everything with love. Our time together began to be filled with ways to encourage and uplift one another . . . I guess what I'm trying to say is we strive for our community life to mirror theirs, by not only adopting their way of life more but also by covering one another with mercy, love, and grace."

Sister Mary Thomas spoke of her own experience: "My first visit to death row showed me that I was not going there to meet criminals, even prisoners, but individual women, human persons, who because of the situation they are in are stripped of all pretense and falsity. In their presence, inhibitions fall, and you are forced to be your true self and not to wear any mask of perfection or superiority." She added: "These women, who have so honestly faced their brokenness and suffering . . . can be an example for all of us. Everyone is tempted in some way by depression, discouragement, or despair, but with Jesus there is always a way out, a way to freedom. Even if that freedom is only in the spirit."

When I think about these encounters between the nuns and the doomed women, I remember that first service I attended with them, on a bright morning in May, after which the inmates invited us to visit their garden. It is something they created together, carving it out of a stretch of the recreation yard between the cell block and the razor wire fence. A trio of stray cats comes to the fence when the ladies are out, expecting to be fed and petted—Tiger, Lover Boy, and Gummy Bear, the last named for his absence of teeth. Doves make their nests in the fence; in the springtime, the chicks will take their first leap into the air, an event the prisoners thrill to.

Several years ago, when the warden permitted the death row women to grow this garden, they weren't allowed to use tools, so they fashioned a plot using rocks, peanut-butter jars, and broken tree limbs. For two hours every day they were able to seed and weed and prune and harvest. It is the only time they are allowed outside, an incredibly precious modicum of freedom. As the warden began to trust the women, the plot expanded to half an acre, aided by the addition of two rototillers, named Rosie and Victoria, and a field cultivator. Deacon Ronnie brings seedlings each season to give the garden a jump-start. "They've got sixty-four tomato plants," he estimated, "probably a hundred and fifty onions, collards, mustard greens, beets, carrots, radishes, just all the varieties of peppers, beans, cantaloupes—" not counting the herbs and flowers.

"It has rained enough to soften the soil, which is something Melissa and I love because it means we can dig," Brittany wrote me that fall. "We are preparing the area where we had the onions to plant okra, so we worked side by side while Darlie tended the tomatoes and Linda swept leaves and dead grass into piles for our newest mulch bed. I looked up as we were working and saw Deacon Ronnie coming in the front gate! He is filling in for our unit chaplain but he came over for a few minutes to say good morning. It was so beautiful out there. Cloudy and breezy which makes working so much easier. I noticed something out of the corner of my eye and looked around. Where I had been tossing clumps of dirt there were two doves carefully picking through it all in search of the perfect twig for their nests, while a few of the grackles were searching for worms.

"This is so much more than a garden. What began as such a small and barren patch, that we dug up with broken sticks and plastic jars, has now become a lush and beautiful garden that stretches from one end of the recreation yard to the other. It is filled with vegetables and herbs of every kind, all growing together in the earth we worked with our own hands.

"For me, it represents my promised land. In so many profound and beautiful ways this is what the Lord has shown me. In it I see the ways he took my brokenness and nurtured it into something able to bear fruit and bring joy. Places my heart had been hardened by things of this world, but he dug deep until those places broke apart and began to sift through his hands. He then planted seeds that took root deep within my heart. As the tiny plants surfaced, new life was revealed."

Sister Mary Thomas noted that the condemned women don't get to enjoy the fruit of their labors. Originally, the officers took home the harvest, but now there is such abundance—more than three hundred pounds of produce a year—that the vegetables serve the entire prison. What moved the sister was that the ladies continue to do the work, regardless of who benefits. "That's part of the abandonment," she said. "You can choose to abandon yourself in an unjust situation. Because the act itself is a beautiful act, they let go of the injustice and continue doing it."

The condemned women were exuberant that morning, dancing between the rows as they showed off the bounty to the nuns. Birdsong filled the air, along with the crack of gunshots from the practice range as the doomed ladies waited for the State of Texas to kill them, one by one.

Afterword

THIS BOOK BEGAN with a walk around Lady Bird Lake in Austin with a longtime friend, Marjorie Clifton. Her mother, Karen, who works with Catholic Prison Ministries, had been to a Mass in the Patrick O'Daniel Unit in Gatesville and learned of the visitations by the Sisters of Mary Morning Star and the role that Deacon Ronnie Lastovica played in making the match. As soon as I returned from my walk with Marjorie, I began to make calls.

I suppose the moral polarity intrigued me—the saintly nuns and the condemned murderers, as I initially conceived it. Perhaps the contrast would provide insight on why people turn their lives toward good or evil. It seemed to me then that there must be life events that marked the turning, and of course some moments in the histories of these women resonate exactly as I expected. Sister Lydia Maria's near-fatal traffic accident led her to make the decision to withdraw from the stimulating material world that she enjoyed, but in the back of her mind was the awareness that her existence lacked meaning. In her telling, the moment of enlightenment happened as the car was knocked off the road and was tumbling over, with death the likely outcome. Her survival gave her the opportunity to take on another existence, to be "reborn" in the evangelical sense.

Most of the women profiled in this book did not have a singular experience that directed the rest of their existence. They lived within the sphere of ordinariness. There were broken families among the nuns and condemned women alike. Most of the women on the row experienced violence in their background. None of the sisters did. Mental illness played a powerful role in Kimberly's life, and I believe is responsible for her cruel behavior toward her family and her chaotic reaction to her babysitter's death. Certainly the volatility of Brittany's childhood shaped her personality and her expectations of what life offered her.

No doubt the extreme abuse Erica suffered, starting in early childhood, contributed to her later behavior, demonstrating again the truth that those who are harmed do harm in return. But not every abused child becomes a killer; in fact, very few do, only more than would be the case if they weren't abused. There must be mitigating factors that enable most wounded children to overcome the scars of their childhood. My amateur observation is that we all seek equilibrium in our lives. A child who has grown up in a loving family is more likely to try to mend the turbulent world he or she may live in as an adult; on the other hand, a child who has experienced violence or sexual assault is more likely to inflict it. These actions, for good or ill, provide a way of harmonizing the inner and outer worlds.

After eleven years working in the prisons full-time, Ronnie Lastovica has retired from active ministry, but he still visits the women on the row. I don't know how he carries the spiritual burden of being exposed to the darkest side of the human experience, but for his sake I'm glad to see it partially lifted from his shoulders.

As of this writing, Brittany's case is still under consideration by the Fifth Circuit Court of Appeals. She published a little volume of her prison homilies, titled *Flowers in the Garden of Mercy*. Melissa Lucio's case is still waiting for final adjudication from the state

Court of Criminal Appeals. This is despite the fact that her attorney, along with the district attorney and the judge in the court in Brownsville, where she was convicted, have all declared her actually innocent.

This book has addressed the question of whether people who have committed heinous crimes can be redeemed. It is a hypothetical question; we can't really know if someone in confinement would revert to criminal behavior if freed into the wider world. I have my own private assessments of the dangerousness of each of the seven women on death row. I can only judge by behavior and what they say about themselves, but there is also the intuitive sense that arises when you perceive someone is lying—to you, or to themselves.

Redemption is finally a religious question. It takes place out of view, inside the heart or soul or mentality of an individual. Most of these women, I believe, have been sufficiently transformed that they can be spared the punishment that society has imposed. But that is not likely to happen.

The question that remains is whether society itself can be redeemed. Justice, in Texas at least, is practiced so casually, with so much prejudice and so little compassion for people, such as Melissa, whose lives are crushed by a state that takes little interest in the consequences of its indifference.

My final visit of 2025—the second year of my trips to the convent and death row—was a few days before Christmas. The O'Daniel Unit was festooned with ribbons and ornaments. The corrections officers wore Santa hats and reindeer antlers. "This time of year can be difficult for the women," the warden told me, and so she countered by stirring up as much seasonal cheer as possible in an institution designed to be joyless and dehumanized. Death row was enrolled in a decoration contest with other units in the prison. With the scarce materials and implements they were allowed, the inmates crafted a giant Santa and a sly, Disneyesque cat—mainly the design of Taylor and Darlie. "We just did what they told us," Brittany said.

A choir of about thirty inmates from general population appeared in the command center lobby to serenade the women on the row. A corrections officer in a Santa outfit and a Grinch mask conducted as they sang "Rockin' Around the Christmas Tree" and "We Wish You a Merry Christmas." The delighted women on the row pressed against the bars to hear. I thought how irrepressible the human spirit can be, how elusive, how it refuses to be wholly confined.

Acknowledgments and Notes on Sources

Throughout my career I've written about closeted worlds. My imagination is invariably drawn to the mystery behind the curtain. That is what led me to write about al-Qaeda, and the world of intelligence, and cults like Scientology. With this story there were two such hidden entities, the convent and death row, neither easy to enter.

That said, the first time I went to Gatesville I walked into the wrong prison. I was buzzed through both gates, and then through the door. A guard asked me to sign in. I asked where I could find the supervisor or warden. "Down the hall and to the right," he said. I thought I followed his instructions but I didn't see any offices. I continued wandering around, finally spotting a line of women at the commissary. I waited with them. When the clerk saw me she asked, "Who are you?"

"I'm a reporter for *The New Yorker*."

"You're not supposed to be here!" she cried.

I had that feeling myself. I worried that getting out would be somewhat more difficult than getting in. Fortunately, a gaggle of what I took to be prison officials were headed out—it was about lunchtime—so I fell in with them and made my escape.

Death row was off-limits to me then. All interviews with the inmates are supposed to be conducted in a room, re-created in so many movies and TV shows, with cubicles on either side of a plexiglass window, and two-way telephones. I spent many one-hour segments interviewing the condemned women on the other side of the window. But the point of the story was to write about the interaction of the nuns and the women on the row, so I had to get inside.

Ronnie Lastovica understood my predicament immediately. He arranged for me to get a pass through the chaplain's office that would grant me access to the row before and after Mass. It was taboo for reporters to go onto the row, so Ronnie asked Chaplain Hazlewood to designate me a "special volunteer." Initially I was to be given four passes onto the row, but when the information office found out a reporter got into death row, that route was blocked. I eventually got another sponsor, Patrick O'Daniel, who permitted me to accompany him on his regular trips to the unit named after him. If it weren't for Ronnie and Patrick, who responded to the spirit of the story, this book could not have been written.

The convent posed another challenge. The nuns of the Sisters of Mary Morning Star are not used to society. They rarely encounter men. And they are silent almost all the time.

Moreover, they harbored a secret: They had fled the dysfunctional Community of Saint John amid charges of sexual predation on the part of the priests. The story was complicated, in part because the sisters claimed that they had not been victims of abuse, but this stance was derided by members of that community and the French Catholic press, who insisted that the nuns were in denial. The Vatican had expelled their order but eventually recognized a new incarnation under another pope. Waco had served as a refuge from those controversies, but now there was an investigative reporter whose curiosity threatened the existence of their order once again.

My goal was not to wreck their lives, but the architecture of the story involved comparing the experiences of the women in the prison with those in the convent. At first, the stories of the nuns were annoyingly bland, but I detected evasiveness when I asked about the background of the order. I picked up the scent. It didn't take long for me to uncover some shocking revelations.

Every reporter faces moments where his reporting can damage individuals he's writing about or people on the sidelines who might be harmed by the information drawn to light. The mission of journalism is to surface the truth, but not every truth needs to be told. I entered into cordial negotiation with Sister Mary Thomas, the vicar of the order, about what I was going to reveal. I allowed her to read the manuscript of this book and offer her suggestions and objections. She was respectful of my obligations to the reader to be straight about what I had learned but offered adjustments to make their ordeal with the church and their former order somewhat less painful.

Each of the women on death row is now well defended, although that wasn't true in the past. Many of these lawyers spent hours explaining their cases to me. Sandra Babcock, Kathrin Schwesinger, David Abernethy, Richard Ellis, Michael Goldberg, Vanessa Potkin, Margaret Smucker, Alice Tsier, Sarah Brandon, Benjamin Wolff, and Alan Wright exemplify the finest expression of American justice. That is not to slight the prosecutors, although in this account the story on them is mixed. I am also grateful to Judge Richard Dambold, in Amarillo, who recounted his experience with Brittany's appeal.

The University of Texas School of Law has been a font of useful sources for me. Jim Marcus, Raoul Schonemann, and Jordan Steiker, who run the Capital Punishment Center, guided me through the fraught world of death penalty law. Jordan did me the favor of reading the manuscript and catching a number of errors. Thea

Posel, a clinical professor at the School of Law as well as the School of Social Work, saved me additional embarrassment. Karen Clifton also read the narrative and provided insight.

Andrea Lozada, a wise and compassionate warden, oversees the O'Daniel Unit. Eric Nichols, head of the Texas Board of Criminal Justice, struck me as an enlightened leader in an organization that is still living down the reputation Texas prisons had back in the *Cool Hand Luke* days of prison management. A living connection to that time is Carlton (C. F.) Hazlewood, the deputy director of religious services for the chaplaincy and volunteer services division of the Texas Department of Criminal Justice. I am grateful for his vivid testimony in this story. I know that I tried the patience of Amanda Hernandez, the director of communications for the prison system. Hannah Haney, the delightful deputy director of that department, was my regular contact, driving back and forth the 160 miles from Huntsville to Gatesville to attend each of my interviews.

Sister Helen Prejean, one of the preeminent opponents of the death penalty, recounted some of the prehistory of the movement. Father Harry Dean Jr. was a frank and delightful informant, as was Bishop Joe Vásquez.

As a journalist, I want to salute my comrade in the trade, Sabrina Van Tassel, for unearthing the scandal that sent Melissa Lucio to death row. Sabrina devoted years to this effort, traveling back and forth from Paris to South Texas, doing the hard work that the Texas criminal justice system should have done when first faced with the case. If it weren't for her, state representatives Toni Rose, Joe Moody, and Jeff Leach would not have had the opportunity to prove themselves the heroes they became.

John Sage and Kelley Meagher Watts opened their hearts to me. I admire their resilience and capacity for forgiveness. They spoke for all the victims of the crimes represented on death row.

Ronnie Lastovica was my guide and advocate throughout this adventure. His wife, Krissie, was an immense help in understanding Ronnie and his ministry.

A portion of this narrative appeared in the 100th Anniversary double issue of *The New Yorker*, February 17 and 24, 2025. I am immensely honored to have been a part of the enterprise for a third of the magazine's distinguished history. I joined the magazine in October 1992, the same month as David Remnick. His leadership through difficult times in journalism, and in our country at large, has kept *The New Yorker* on course. Daniel Zalewski, a cherished friend, has been my editor for most of that time. Teresa Mathew and Jackson Vail were the scrupulous fact-checkers for the story. Any errors that remain are my fault.

Katy Grannan, one of America's greatest photographers, contributed the formal portraits of the women and the nuns that grace this book.

Sharp-eyed biblical scholars might notice that my quotes from scripture do not all come from the same translation. Some verses read better in the traditional King James Version, others in the New Oxford or the Catholic edition of the New Revised Standard Version. I allowed myself to choose the most expressive among them.

Knopf has been my home through many books. I have the good fortune to work once again with my editor, Peter Gethers, on this one. The Knopf team includes Chip Kidd, who designed the jacket (as he has so often on previous books); Erinn Hartman, the head of publicity; Claire Leonard, who did the legal read; Hilary Redmon, the editorial director of nonfiction; Gabrielle Brooks, the associate publisher; and Jordan Pavlin, the publisher.

Not all the nuns wished to be interviewed. I am indebted to Sisters Jeanne Thomas, Mary Guadalupe, Pia Maria, Eva Nella, Lydia Maria, and Mary Thomas. They emerged from seclusion to take on a task they could never have expected when they accepted their orders. I am fond of these women. They were kind to me and surprisingly full of joy.

Pam Perillo, who spent forty years incarcerated in Texas, talked movingly about her experience—not only her time on death row, but her disorienting adjustment to freedom.

Finally, there are the women who still wait for death. It took time for some of them to agree to meet with me. I posed a threat to them. I might write something that would tip the scales in their appeals or awaken a district attorney to the duty of seeking an execution date. Families of the victims might be stirred to protest. When I drove to Gatesville for my first interview in March 2024, I arrived to find that the two women I was supposed to interview had changed their minds. I drove back to Austin, contemplating the possibility that I would never gain the trust I needed to write this story. I considered what I might do if my life were in jeopardy and talking to a reporter might be a fatal decision. Each of these women overcame her reluctance. I end with thanks to Kimberly Cargill, Linda Carty, Brittany Holberg, Melissa Lucio, Taylor Parker, Darlie Routier, and Erica Sheppard. I wish them all a long life.

A NOTE ABOUT THE AUTHOR

LAWRENCE WRIGHT is a staff writer for *The New Yorker* and the author of eleven works of nonfiction and four novels. His books have received many honors, including the Pulitzer Prize for *The Looming Tower: Al-Qaeda and the Road to 9/11*. He is also a playwright and screenwriter. He and his wife are longtime residents of Austin, Texas.

A NOTE ON THE TYPE

This book was set in Monotype Dante, a typeface designed by Giovanni Mardersteig (1892–1977). Conceived as a private type for the Officina Bodoni in Verona, Italy, Dante was originally cut for hand composition by Charles Malin, the famous Parisian punch cutter, between 1946 and 1952. Its first use was in an edition of Boccaccio's *Trattatello in laude di Dante* that appeared in 1954. The Monotype Corporation's version of Dante followed in 1957. Although modeled on the Aldine type used for Pietro Cardinal Bembo's treatise *De Aetna* in 1495, Dante is a thoroughly modern interpretation of the venerable face.

Composed by North Market Street Graphics,
Lancaster, Pennsylvania

Designed by Cassandra J. Pappas